Blood, Sweat and Suspenders

Blood, Sweat and Suspenders

ANDREA ASTON ORME

StoryTerrace

Text Andrea Orme
Copyright © Andrea Aston Orme

First print July 2024

www.StoryTerrace.com

CONTENTS

CHAPTER ONE: AND SO IT BEGINS...   9

CHAPTER TWO: STUPID SKOOL   15

CHAPTER THREE: SAUCY AWAKENINGS   25

CHAPTER FOUR: FAMILY MATTERS AND CHICKEN HEAD BRIAN   31

CHAPTER FIVE: OLDER MEN AND WASHING MACHINES   39

CHAPTER SIX: MICHAEL AND I GO ESCORTING   45

CHAPTER SEVEN: DANGEROUSLY HIGH WINDS!   53

CHAPTER EIGHT: A MEXICAN ADVENTURE   57

CHAPTER NINE: HOME SWEET HOME AND A NEW SALON   67

CHAPTER TEN: LIFE WITH KEITH AND A CHANCE ENCOUNTER   73

CHAPTER ELEVEN: MOPS, MOWERS AND A REVOLUTIONARY IDEA	79
CHAPTER TWELVE: TIFFANY AND JANE CARRY ON AGAIN	85
CHAPTER THIRTEEN: ABSOLUTE STUNNERS	93
CHAPTER FOURTEEN: PHIL'S A TWAT	101
CHAPTER FIFTEEN: DARK DAYS IN CAMBRIDGE	105
CHAPTER SIXTEEN: LIFE WITH BLOSSOM WAS NOT BLOSSOMING	113
CHAPTER SEVENTEEN: A FABULOUSLY SAD SEND-OFF	119
CHAPTER EIGHTEEN: THE PINK BOA AND A PSYCHOPATH, LYING PIECE OF RUBBISH	123
CHAPTER NINETEEN: UNUSUAL HOMES AND CURIOUS KINKS	131
CHAPTER TWENTY: LIVING AND LEARNING	135

CHAPTER ONE: AND SO IT BEGINS...

My goal in publishing this book is to provide readers with an honest glimpse into my world. Over the decades, I've donned many guises, but for far too long I obscured my truest self in secrecy and shame. I believe in opening hearts and minds through openness and empathy and my unconventional life is not so different from anyone else's when you look at our shared hopes, fears and dreams.

In these pages, you'll ride shotgun as I career through all my adventures and misadventures, joining me at the crossroads where I made brave choices and cowardly mistakes. Unlike my father, I'll break the silence wide open and speak my whole truth as this story belongs to me and me alone, though it never would have unfolded without the cast of colourful characters that have paraded through my life.

So, find a cosy nook, pour yourself a cuppa and join me on an unusual trip you won't soon forget. Just be forewarned dears, things are going to get fabulous!

*

It all started on Thursday 5th November 1959, at 7:30 in the morning. I was born at home, in the front bedroom, with just a midwife by my mother's side as my father was at work. My father and I were never close, as I was never quite what he wanted, so I suppose things started as they meant to go on...

My earliest memory from those days is of sitting on the back of Mum's bicycle, on a child seat, feeling very unsafe – a feeling which basically carried on throughout my whole life. I've never felt safe and secure. Mum told me that she didn't want more children after my sister, Carol, was born, so she sat in a hot bath and drank a bottle of gin to try and get rid of me, but I'm not sure whether she should have told me that…

My maternal nan, born in 1902, lived next door to us when I was little and she was a kind, caring woman who did provide me with some sense of love and security. Her name was Mabel, like my mother, and I loved her garden full of flowers, and a greenhouse that smelt beautiful and weird at the same time. She could plant anything and it would grow, my nan… I think I take after her in that way. I also have her legs; good strong legs with no varicose veins!

As an added bonus, she worked in a cake shop, which was great news for me as, most Saturdays, she brought lots of lovely cakes home! I was very glad of my nan's presence in my life when I was young, along with the company of my assortment of animals: hamsters, guinea pigs, tortoises and even a snail called Touchwood. My first dog was called Penny after my mother's Surname, Pen.

My second memory is of hiding behind a chair at home, with Mum then grabbing me and dragging me out the front door to start at the infants' school, which was on the same road. She later said that I'd kicked the secretary there so hard that it took weeks for the bruises to go down, but that, I don't remember, which is convenient. I do remember a friend I had in the infants called Dawn, who used to do my shoes up, so I guess we must have got on well and I must have made at least one friend. After a while, the staff wrote a letter to my mother: 'We believe your son is deaf and dumb because in six months he's not said a word.' But I wasn't deaf and dumb, I just didn't want to be there.

I was an introverted, gentle child who shunned the rough and tumble of the playground, preferring creative solo pursuits like colouring and imaginative roleplay. The differences between Carol's personality and my own were clearly defined right from the start.

By the time I started primary school, my parents' marriage had deteriorated significantly; my father craved the stereotypical boisterous, sporty son and lost patience with my shy, artistic temperament. Aloof by nature, he had little idea how to connect emotionally with a child like me. His disappointment was evident in the long, disapproving silences, lack of physical affection and criticism of everything that mattered to me, from keeping pets to looking at the pictures in books and playing with my Action Man doll (because I liked his muscles...)

My mother did her best to protect and nurture me but lacked the assertiveness to stand up to my father's old-fashioned beliefs. She poured all her thwarted creative energies into the home, making sure meals were served on time and keeping our little house spotless. A gifted amateur flower arranger, she briefly had a part-time job doing the teas at my school, but could not manage regular work due to my father's domestic expectations.

Money was scarce despite my father's insurance job. Major purchases like our first television set required endless saving schemes and new clothes were rare treasures doled out for birthdays and Christmas. We always had food on the table and a roof over our heads, but there was no room for frivolity.

My father allocated my mother a stingy housekeeping allowance, scrutinising every penny spent, so she took to hiding small change around the house, concealing it inside empty candle jars and film canisters. More than once I glimpsed her covertly counting pennies onto the counter when she thought I wasn't looking, her face creased with worry. I'd quickly retreat before she realised I was there, wanting to spare her embarrassment. The path that led me from a shy schoolboy to the accomplished lady I am today was often a rocky one, yet the difficulties I faced also made me resilient, empathetic and open to new possibilities. My story was just beginning...

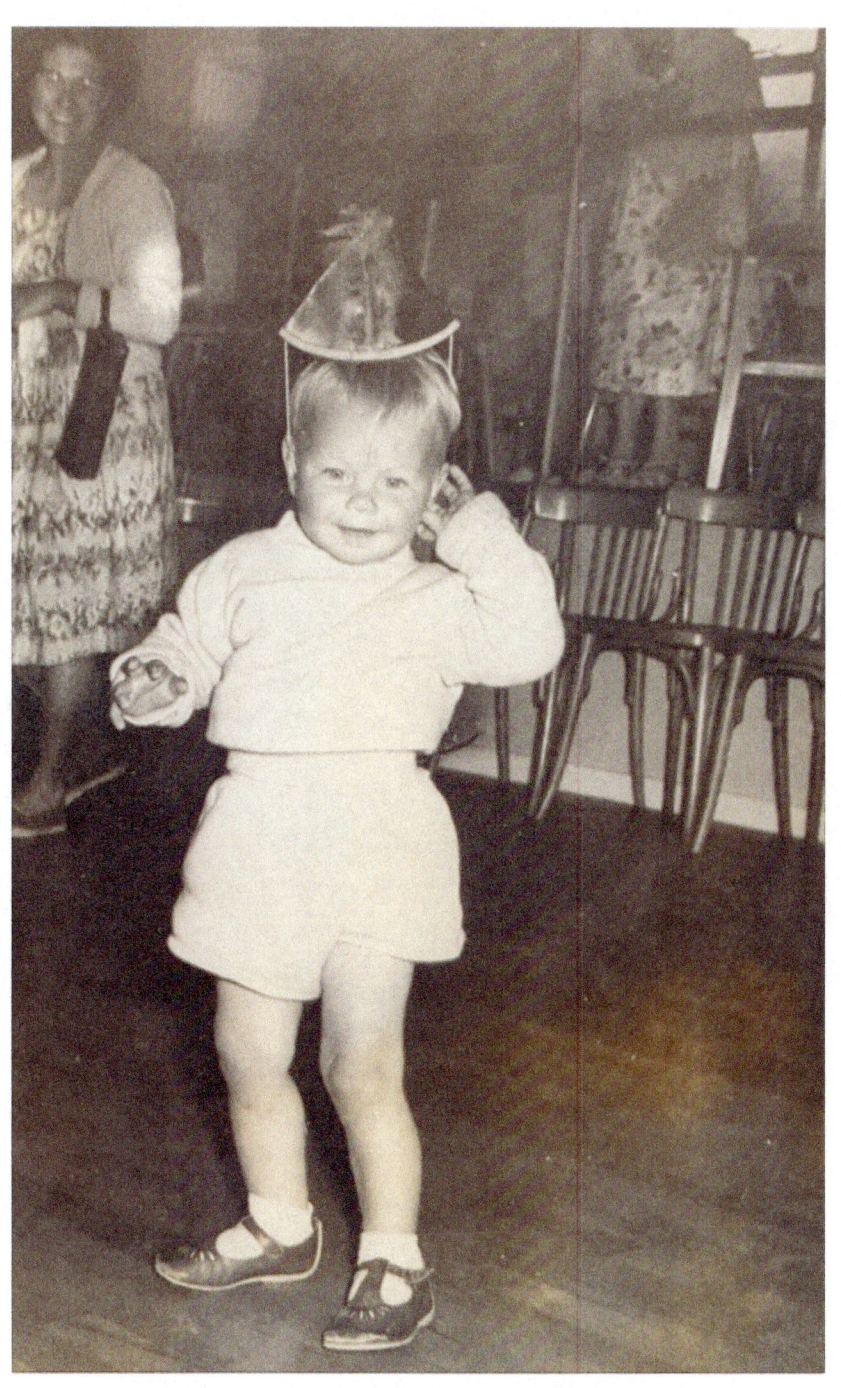

Me in 1961 mum is in the background I have a party hat on, I still wear hats.

The house on the left is the house I was born in. 1959 My nan lived next door.

CHAPTER TWO: STUPID SKOOL

At around the age of eight, Mum took me to a special school in town – I didn't know why I was going to a special school – but we sat there patiently, waiting for the head teacher. There was a boy with Down syndrome in the waiting room with us and I'd never seen someone like that before, so, as a child, I remember being quite frightened. He actually turned out to be the teacher's son. I didn't attend this school as it turned out; partly because Mum would have had to take-on more jobs to pay for it and partly because I never wanted to go there anyway.

As far as school was concerned, I hated every single minute of it. It was very hard work for me... and being dyslexic and slightly number blind, I just used to sit there, looking at the blackboard in front of me, not understanding a thing and wondering what was going on. Most of the time, I just used to stare out of the window.

Back in the 1960s, students with learning difficulties like mine were simply written off as dim-witted and unteachable. I clearly recall sitting at the back of the classroom, staring vacantly out the window while the clever kids up front answered the teacher's questions. The words on the blackboard may as well have been hieroglyphics for all the sense they made to me. My school reports invariably described me as a 'dreamer' who lacked focus and discipline.

If only they had realised I wasn't daydreaming out of laziness, but simply couldn't understand the lessons! The teachers meant well, but special educational support for dyslexics like myself was virtually non-existent at the time.

I hated all sports, especially football, and diving for a ball in a goal on the concrete. The PE teacher used to say, 'Come on boys! Let's get out and play football; and you, Orme!' They'd toss a coin to see who would have to have me in their team. I didn't like swimming either, particularly as it was in an outside pool, so my mother gave me a note saying I had a verruca. I used that note for two years…

When I was 12 I contracted a severe case of glandular fever. The exhaustion hit me hard and I would drag myself home from school each day and head straight to bed, only to wake up drenched in sweat a few hours later. The doctors feared it could be something more sinister like Hodgkin's lymphoma, so they scheduled me for surgery to remove one of the swollen lymph nodes for testing. I'll never forget sitting in that cold, clinical room in my paper gown awaiting the biopsy results. The relief when they confirmed it was just run-of-the-mill glandular fever was immense, but the extreme fatigue persisted for years afterwards. I'd be playing with friends after school and have to leave abruptly, the tiredness washing over me in crushing waves. Richard and Paul never teased me for it, though. They were true friends.

My lack of sporting prowess hardly helped matters at secondary school; whilst the other boys eagerly discussed football scores or boasted about their rugby tackles, I stood on the sidelines, a gangly daydreamer uninterested in chasing balls through the mud.

Another early memory is of my brief stint with the Cubs. In keeping with traditional gender roles, my father hoped I would grow into a sporty, rough-and-tumble boy. He had been mad about cricket, football and rugby in his youth, so I think he envisioned us kicking a ball about together as father and son. The reality was that I loathed any form of strenuous physical activity or competitive sport. When I came home from school covered in scrapes and bruises, it was invariably because I'd fallen over my own feet, not from fighting with other boys. Still, my parents enrolled me in Cubs, hoping to toughen me up.

It was a disaster from the word 'go.' At my first meeting, I was terrified to stand up in front of the group to recite the Cub Scout Promise. I've always suffered from crippling stage fright, even now as an adult. My hands shook so badly I could barely hold the sheet of paper with the words written on it. I stammered and stuttered, my childish voice quivering until I finally gave up halfway through. The other boys sat cross-legged on the floor, staring up at me in bemusement. After that humiliation, things only got worse. A typical Cub activity was piggyback fighting, where you had to sit on another boy's shoulders and try to wrestle opponents off their perch onto the hard concrete floor. The very thought made me shudder. After only two or three weeks, I told my parents I was quitting and never returned. It was abundantly clear that I'd never make it as a Cub Scout.

My father made no secret of his disappointment in me. Frankly, I think he considered me somewhat of a failure right from the start. All he cared about was sports and manly pursuits like fishing, neither of which held the slightest bit of interest for me. When he was home, he basically ignored my existence unless I'd done something to earn his scorn, like failing to clean my plate at dinner or tracking mud inside the house. Even as a young child, I knew he saw me as an irritation rather than someone to nurture and bond with as his son. I can't recall him ever praising me for anything or expressing the slightest bit of affection.

When the day came, I started at senior school and for this arduous task, I had to catch a bus. I had to walk about a mile up to the shopping centre in Rayners Lane, Harrow, and it was the 98B bus as I recall. It was an extremely old vehicle, from just after the war, and although there was a more modern one, the H1, I was happy to be on the 98B as it took slightly longer to get to school, which gave me more time to smoke cigarettes. I used to smoke Number Six with my best friend, Richard, who I used to do everything with back then… and I mean, everything. We used to play saucy doctors and nurses (if you know what I mean) and our secret word for it was 'go-karts.'

Richard provided some respite from the trials of school, and we shared the same offbeat sense of humour and taste in music. I'll never forget the time his dad borrowed an army tank and let us ride along – sticking our heads out the top to wave at bemused motorists, our laughter echoing across the countryside, or the mischievous pranks we pulled like waiting for old ladies to walk by so we could slap their bottoms and run off howling with laughter. Such carefree antics are the preserve of teenage boys, I suppose. We pushed the boundaries at every turn. One summer we progressed from knocking on front doors to tapping hats, picking increasingly grumpy gentlemen to target each day. I had the rotten luck to choose an Olympic marathon runner once; who chased me for a mile, rage blazing in his eyes. I collapsed on our front steps afterwards, lungs burning and legs trembling, the threat of a heart attack the only thing placating my fury at Richard and Paul's howls of laughter.

Surviving those tricky teenage years made me who I am today but it came at a high price. Dyslexia, my father's emotional abuse and feeling like a misfit at school left scars that have never fully healed. To this day, I still struggle badly with reading, writing and maths. Simple tasks like following a new recipe or reading a map leave me terribly anxious. I'm convinced people will judge me as stupid or lazy, just like my teachers did all those years ago. It takes real courage for me to ask for help when I'm struggling to understand something in everyday life. Understandably, I'm also wary of getting close to romantic partners after growing up in such an unaffectionate, troubled household.

My childhood and adolescence were far from easy, yet those difficulties shaped me in ways I'm proud of too. I learned resilience in the face of hardship and hostility. I discovered creativity and independence could be powerful tools of self-expression. And I know first-hand how small acts of tenderness, like my nan welcoming me in when the yelling got too much at home, can make all the difference in a young life.

Mum and dads wedding in Pinner Middlesex 1952.

Mum at 17 I think she looked like the Queen

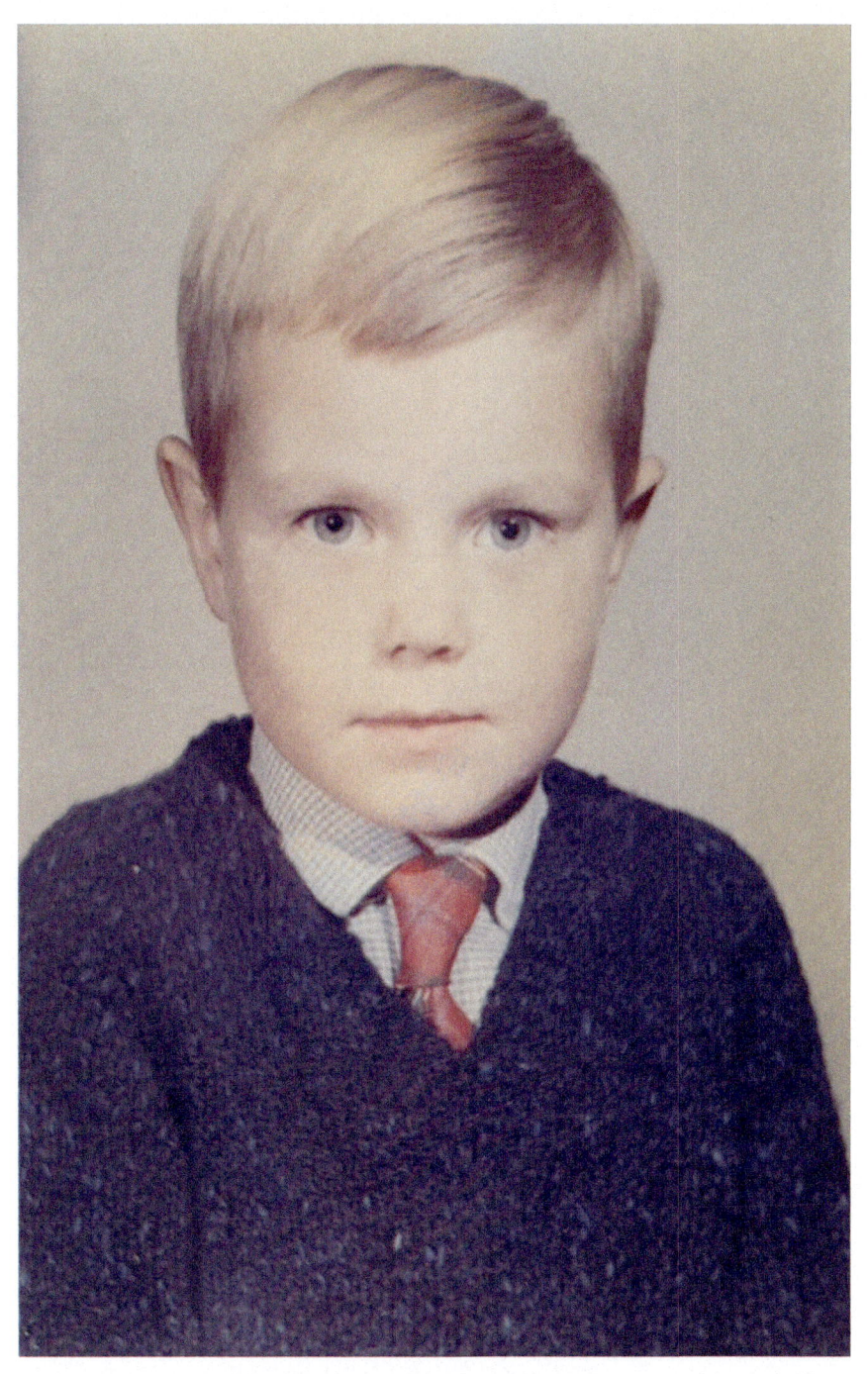

School photo they say I was as I looked (shy)

CHAPTER THREE: SAUCY AWAKENINGS

In my very last year of school, something changed in me, and the summer holiday before the last term, I became a big fan of David Bowie. I even had my hair cut like him, which annoyed my father intensely, to the point where he even started threatening to cancel our holiday that year! When I came back from the hairdressers, Mum cried, 'Oh my God, David! Do something with it!' It was all standing up on top, so I dutifully put some water on it, which made it go flat.

At the age of 15, my sister introduced me to some teenagers, college boys as I recall, and they were making a film all about a newspaper called *The Day in the Life of a Paper*. It was about someone buying it in a shop and its journey throughout the day, all the way up until a tramp was sleeping on it in the evening. I had fun doing the hair and makeup for them, and my father actually had a part in it! I think he was sitting on a bench reading it and then putting it in the dustbin…

As a teenager, I got a job in an off licence in the High Street on Rayners Lane, and a man used to come in every so often called John, who started chatting me up. He worked for EMI in Golden Square, London and he actually became a very important person in my life story because he's the one who took my life in a completely different direction. I was just a young boy at the time I met him, going to school and working in an off licence, but John started taking me to places like The Royal Vauxhall Tavern, which was the first adult nightspot I'd ever been to at that point. Thanks to John, I met many new people and my life started to take off.

He worked in the cinema on the opposite side of the road at the weekends, and I felt there was something different between me and John. He kept looking at me intently, smiling and talking and said that if I wanted to go to the cinema, he could get me in for free. I had very little money at the time, so that was a rather good offer, and I went along.

The film was *The Jungle Book* (the original) and I remember being there with John after Christmas, when he told me he knew David Bowie! That was like a fishing hook to a rather naïve teenage fish, so I stayed behind in the secretive darkness of the cinema and all we could see were the cigarettes and their little wisps of smoke rising into the air. I was only 15 and a half at the time and I nervously tried to tell John I'd put some weight on over Christmas, but before I knew it, his hands were inside my trousers. That became my first oral experience, and also my first orgasm, and I even broke the seats in front as my leg shot out in ecstasy!

I have to say, I did go back a couple of times that week to see 'the film' again, but John didn't stop there. He took me to The Royal Vauxhall Tavern, around the time of New Year I think it was, and I remember there being a lot of decorations and balloons. I was petrified back then because the only gay people I had ever encountered were people on tele, people in TV sitcoms such as *Are You Being Served?* John was OK though and my mother wanted to meet him after a while because I'd started going out in the evening, which was something I hadn't done before. Thankfully, she thought he was all right because he was wearing a nice suit and lived with his mother.

He introduced me to Peter Wyngarde, the famous actor who appeared in popular television shows of the day, such as *The Avengers*, *The Saint*, *The Prisoner* and *Department S*. I met him in his flat somewhere in London, and we drank champagne from very long fluted glasses. He looked exactly like he did on the tele! Then he said, 'Do you want to meet Danny LaRue?'

'No, thank you.' I replied.

Rayners lane Harrow the cinema far right where I had my first sexual experience. 1975.

Mum me Carol Auntie Doll Don 1980 in Hythe Kent the miniature railway went passed, I had great times there on the canal.

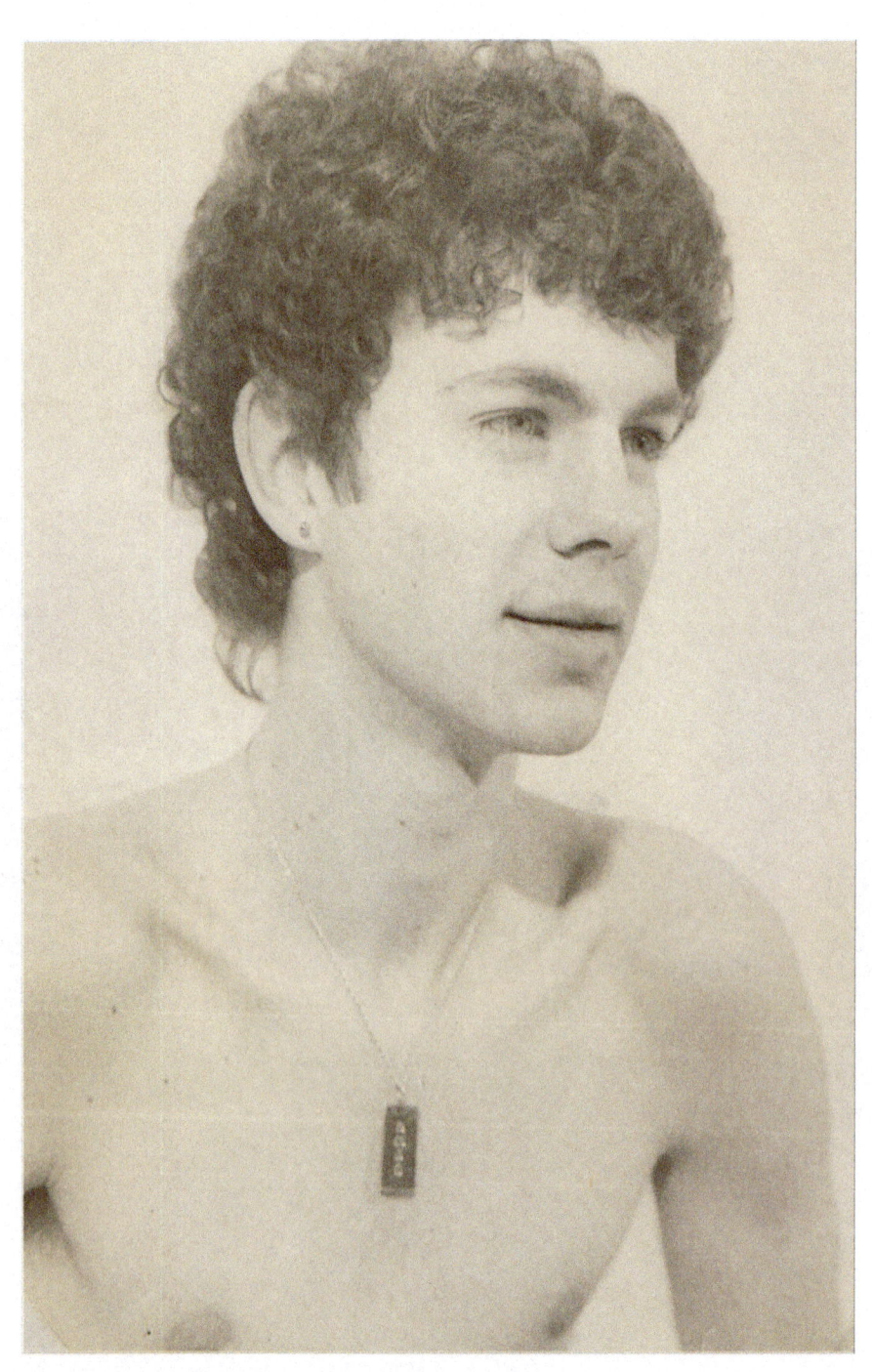

Me in 1975 with a perm. Perms were in.

CHAPTER FOUR: FAMILY MATTERS AND CHICKEN HEAD BRIAN

My father and mother were getting close to divorcing during my teenage years, so things were very rocky at home. Personally, I don't think they should have gotten married in the first place. They had few shared interests – my father was into sport and my mother was into flower arranging – but in the end, it transpired that there had been much more serious issues as Mum eventually divorced Dad on the grounds of mental cruelty and rape.

Carol and I are five years apart so we didn't do a lot of things together, although she had a boyfriend called Henry – an American who played in a band – so she actually invited me up to London on one occasion, to watch him perform in Notting Hill Gate. We were in the pub and I remember suddenly being herded off to the basement where we remained for about 10 or 15 minutes. The reason why finally became clear when we heard the sound of an enormous explosion from up above, and we found out later that a bomb had gone off across the road, killing a policeman. This was in about 1975 and once it was all over the news, it turned out that IRA bombers were responsible for the attack.

My sister didn't get on with our father either. I think a clash of personalities was the main cause, but I can recall how she threw an ashtray at him once when she was about 18, then left the house and secured herself a little flat and a job with British Airways. I was still at home, obviously, but divorce was in the air and the house was more or less split in two. My father had the heating controls so we only had heat when he was in, which meant that life at home was pretty dark and stressful, to say the least.

At this point, I met a guy from Holland called Brian, who used to make mosaics and had a dog called Jenny. Brian and I engaged in a lot of different sexual acts and indulged in a lot of weed smoking, although there was a huge age difference between us as I was still only 16 and he was nearly 40. We used to listen to Pink Floyd and Simon & Garfunkel and I remember it being a fun time, although I used to have to get the bus to go and see him and as there were no mobile phones in those days, I had to go to a telephone box if we needed to arrange a meet-up or have a chat. Despite the age difference, I can't forget the feeling of incredible excitement that I got from this relationship and the nervousness of calling him on the phone.

I stayed over one evening and we spent the time drinking and smoking, which was normal enough, but when I went to the toilet and sat down, I happened to look between my knees and there was a chicken's head looking up at me! Why on earth would anyone in their right mind chop off a chicken's head and put it down the toilet!? I nearly took off with fright!

Even though he seemed like a nice man, there was clearly another more disturbing side to him.

A friend came and picked me up and took us both to a mobile home with people my age and younger, hanging out with older men. I was not told at the time, but I have thought about this over the years; about whether they were paedophiles. I cannot remember clearly what happened as I know we were smoking quite a lot of weed, so I wonder whether we were drugged with something heavier.

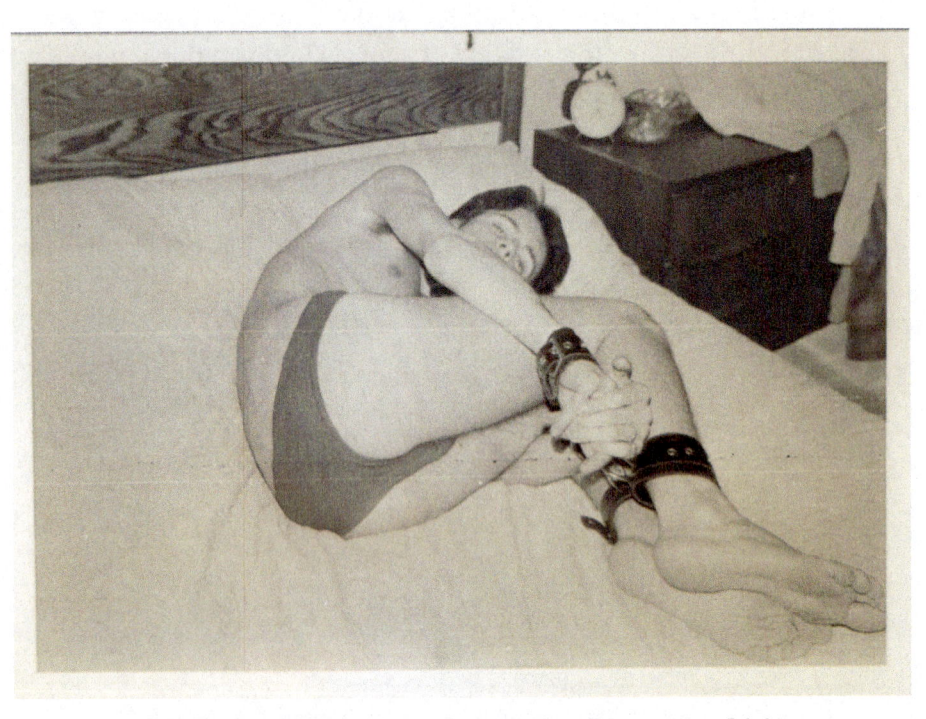

1975 Peter the CID Officer was teaching me to drive. Payment was me I do have more photos but I think one is enough.

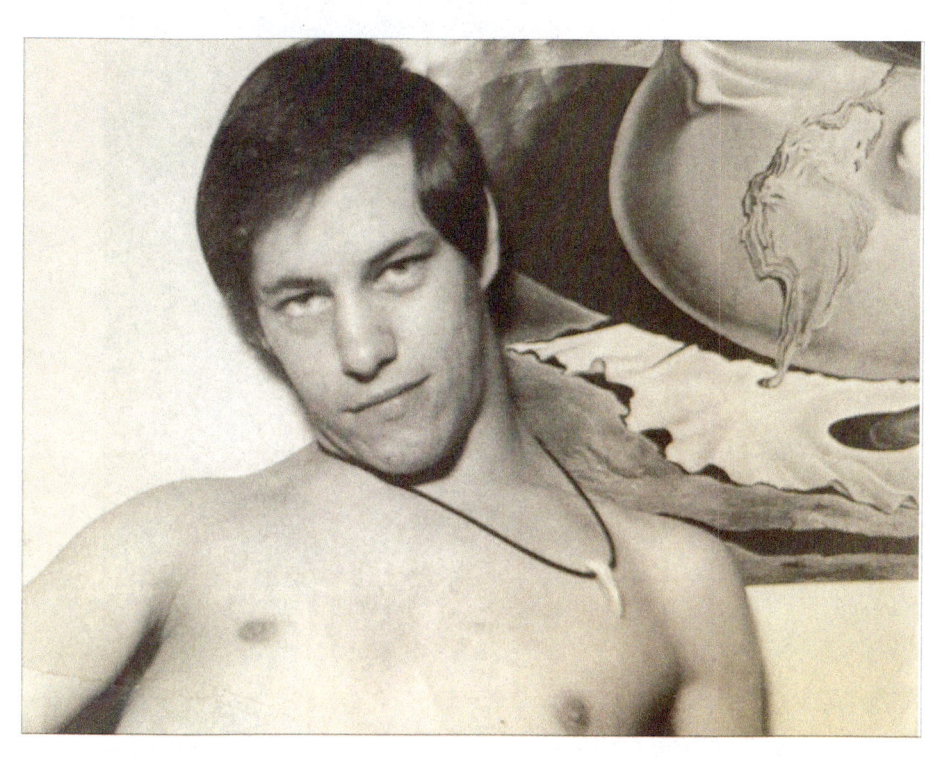

Best friend Michael 1976 looking hot there X

Louise she stayed with Mike and me in 1977 for about 9 months she was an escort working in London clubs. She was fun. XX

Mike and me in the Black Cap 1977 in Camden Town, I love this photo, miss you lots XX

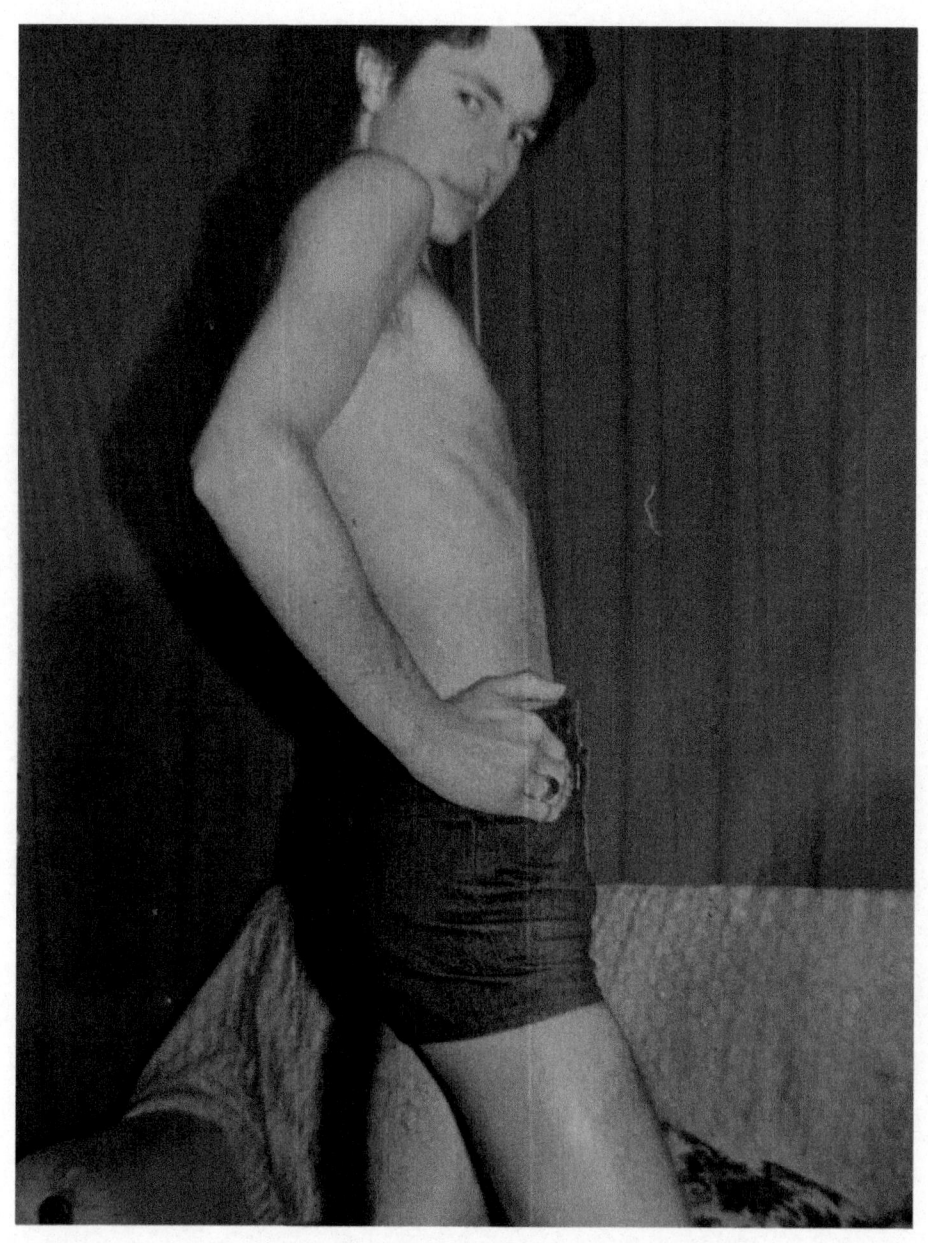

16 and slim this is when the CID guy took photographs of me

CHAPTER FIVE: OLDER MEN AND WASHING MACHINES

Leaving school and entering the workforce was both exciting and intimidating. On one hand, I was thrilled to be done with classrooms and eager to start earning my own money, but on the other, the prospect of finding a career and being a responsible adult seemed daunting. Though I had no clear direction yet, I knew I wanted a job I was passionate about.

My passion at the time was hair and beauty, and as a teenager, I started experimenting with dramatic makeup looks and styling my friends' hair for school dances. I just found the whole process creative and fun, so after finishing school, becoming a professional hairdresser felt like a natural fit. Luckily, my mother found me the job at David Barrie in Kenton which was a train ride about four stops from Rayners Lane, and it was a very high class salon.

On my first day, the owner, Mr David, a real gentleman, gave me a brief tour of where we wash hair and where we sweep up the cut hair. I smiled and nodded, eager to prove myself, and the other hairdressers, all women except for Mr David, regarded me warmly. I could tell they were amused by my enthusiasm, but unfortunately for me, as Mr David owned the salon, and as my name was also David, I had to be called Lloyd, my middle name, which I hated.

To start, I was tasked with menial jobs like sweeping floors, taking out trash and sterilising combs. But I didn't mind. Just being in that creative environment made me feel like I was part of something special. I watched the seasoned stylists carefully, trying to absorb their techniques. An older hairdresser assured me I'd get my chance with the scissors soon.

When I wasn't at the salon, I attended hairdressing college once a week. The classes covered everything from the proper use of clippers to the chemistry behind perms and dyes. Thanks to my dyslexia, the textbook portions gave me trouble. I had to read chapters over and over, deciphering each word, but the practical lessons were a delight. I'd leave class twirling my mannequin's lush locks, imagining the day clients would request me as their stylist.

Within a few months, I was granted small responsibilities like blow-drying regulars' hair. I was meticulous, not wanting to disappoint Mr David or the customers. My first opportunity to actually cut came one afternoon when the salon was slow. My hand trembled slightly as I tied the nylon cape around the woman's neck. I could tell the other hairdressers were watching, which only increased my nerves.

But muscle memory from college kicked in. I carefully combed her hair, still damp from the wash, and made my first tentative snip. The rest of the trim flowed smoothly, just like I'd practised hundreds of times. I was bursting with pride when I finished. After that, opportunities to style regulars' hair increased. I relished the connections I formed with clients as I worked, chatting while colours set or rollers were in.

Chicken Head Brian introduced me to Philip and another Brian who was a car mechanic, and they were both a lot older than me. Philip was in his 30s and the other Brian was in his 40s, but they both seemed nice, although Brian seemed a bit rough and Philip seemed a little bit nervous. As I was still training at the hairdressers back then and as the college was quite near to Philip's flat, he used to cook me dinner from time to time and we used to visit a pub in Hampstead called the William IV, as well as a couple of other bars. They used to buy all the drinks - I think I was basically the payment for all the food and drink - but I remember noticing that Philip was very well-endowed when we were back in his flat together. Sometimes I slept with both of them and I started taking what they offered me, sexually.

Then they introduced me to a man called Peter, a CID policeman and a sadist. He said he'd teach me to drive on private land as I was still 16 and not yet old enough to go out on the roads, but what I remember most about Peter is that he had incredible eyebrows, a lot like Dennis Healey! On one occasion, while we were out driving on this area of private land, the police arrived and asked Peter what we were doing, but after he got out of the car and spoke to them for a couple of minutes, they just saluted him and drove off!

Back at Philip's flat, Peter tied me up, severely spanked my bottom and then forced me to have sex. On top of that, he then told me he was married. It was the first time I had ever had such an unpleasant experience. Philip and Brian were very scared of him and I think they were quite concerned about me, so, in the end, I only saw Peter on one more occasion and that was it. I continued seeing Philip and Brian for about six months or so, but before I met them, I do remember a short relationship I had with a seven-foot-tall Selfridges security guard named Richard who I'd met in a pub when I was celebrating my birthday. Richard was the first person I ever really had sex with and he was big, in every way you can think of, but he was nice. He was adopted and lived at home, and my mother liked him which was a bonus.

The day of my parents' divorce arrived whilst I was working in Kenton and seeing Richard, and my mum and I had to leave the house, although my father, obstinate as ever, insisted on keeping the washing machine.

My mother and I had very little money, although luckily Mum had managed to buy a small flat in South Ruislip, but I said to Richard, 'We really need the washing machine! We can't afford one.'

'Don't worry,' Richard replied, and he arrived at our old home with two very large friends in tow. They rang the doorbell, I opened it, and then these three monsters walked in, leaving my father completely powerless to do anything. I was hoping he was going to try to be honest because they would have squashed him!

I said goodbye to my dog, Penny, which was very sad, and then my father closed the door on us, leaving us to head off to our new flat. I carried on seeing Richard for about six months after this, and visiting him in the home he shared with his adoptive parents, but unfortunately I found out that he used to frequent nearly every public toilet in London! So I got rid of him. I carried on hairdressing until I had qualified, but through Richard there was at least one silver lining as I met Michael, who became my best friend for over 30 years.

Dads 3rd marriage to Beryl I was best man and that's my car. She was sweet, it lasted 2 years.

CHAPTER SIX: MICHAEL AND I GO ESCORTING

Michael worked in Selfridges, in the china department, and for some reason, we became just friends. He moved in with me and my mother for about seven months while we were waiting for a flat to open up on Finchley Road, near Hampstead, but when the day came to move in, I felt like my life had really started to take off. I had very little money and Michael earned more than I did – I was only on £20.50 per week – but we loved going out and about together. We decided to have a party on one occasion, even though we didn't know many people, but Michael said, 'Let's phone one of the clubs!'

It turned out to be a bikers' club, and they made an announcement over the Tannoy, which resulted in 200 leather-clad bikers turning up on our doorstep! It was only a humble one-bedroom flat with a small living room, kitchen and bathroom, but suddenly, on that eventful evening in 1977, there was a whole street full of Harley-Davidsons on the outside of the building and an enormous amount of sex going on inside! There was a guy rolling joints all night, and people having sex in the bath and using the toilet at the same time!

Michael had done a bit of escorting a few years before I met him, and he suggested that if we wanted to have more money to play with, I give it a go. It was new to me, but I thought, 'Better than giving it away, I might as well get paid for it!' So, we got dressed in our finest clothes – modern youngsters' clothes – and went down to Piccadilly station.

I was nearly 17 when I started escorting in Piccadilly Station, and I'll always remember this Asian man coming up to me asking if I would have sex with his wife. I remember thinking, 'What!? You're mad! No! Why are you asking me?' But it's actually happened many, many times since then, not just from Asian men, but men of every shape, size and colour. I've always said no.

Upstairs at Piccadilly Station was a circle with the ticket office and things in the middle, and Michael and I just used to walk around. There were no cameras in those days, although there were some police, but they never bothered us, perhaps because we were clean and tidy, unlike the boys they stopped who were dirty and ill-looking. Very quickly I got good at spotting 'the look' which told me that somebody wanted to have sex, and I would wait for them up the stairs at the station and we would both go to the hotel or flat together. You learned very quickly if someone was looking at you with sex in mind, how to discern a mere glance of interest from a desirous stare within milliseconds, and this skill was crucial to selecting the right clients. With so many unsavoury characters frequenting Piccadilly, one had to be choosy. Cleanliness in the 70s and 80s wasn't high on men's list of priorities and quite a lot of them were quite unclean, unsavoury, and when we first started doing escorting in the late 70s Michael and myself requested appointments at the clinic on a fairly regular basis. Everything was cured by a handful of tablets. and most of the guys were active, meaning they were 'tops'; they did you. Back then, anything could happen once alone with a stranger, but thankfully we remained unscathed during those precarious early days.

After my parents divorce, I didn't see my dad again for another 15 years, but my mum was proud that I'd worked hard at my hairdressing studies, and she was pleased that at least I was not sitting around idle. High praise from her! By the time I reached the end of my three-year apprenticeship, I had had regular salon clients requesting me as their designated stylist, and my confidence and skill with the shears had increased exponentially from that first shaky trim. I had still got nervous occasionally, trying a new technique or working with long hair, which took more precision, but I had loved the creativity and helping ladies leave looking and feeling their best.

It was a proud moment when I received my certification and our hairdressing college held an awards ceremony, announcing the top students in different categories. I can still picture clutching the paper certificate, so thrilled that my effort was finally recognised. My difficulties with schoolwork seemed less painful, knowing I had a real talent to pursue. I went back to hairdressing time and time again over the years and I never completely lost my passion for it, but at the end of the day, escorting paid more and was more exciting. It was a lot more fun, so even after qualifying and getting two credits and a distinction – the best in the year and in my salon (and the only thing I'd ever passed) - as well as an honourable mention from the director in front of all the apprentices and instructors – we carried on escorting.

Escorting opened up a whole new world to me. The clandestine late nights meeting all manner of men were often an adrenaline rush and I enjoyed entering fine hotels, even if just briefly. These outings provided glitzy experiences far beyond my limited teenage horizons.

As my confidence grew, escorting propelled me from the shy boy next door into an urbane, sexually liberated young man. I blossomed under the simple positive reinforcement of so many men desiring my company, even if it was primarily physical. The male attention I had craved for so long was now amply provided, along with a decent income.

My youth quickly made me one of the most requested escorts and although this was good in many ways, it also brought its fair share of drama. Jealousy issues plagued many of my relationships during this period and boyfriends and clients alike bristled as I constantly attracted admirers. I hadn't yet learned to establish firm boundaries in relationships, but after weathering so many tempestuous affairs, I eventually acquired that ability.

During my late teenage years and early 20s, escorting afforded me freedom and adventure. As the saying goes, I was growing up fast. But soon even more complications and challenges awaited. The glamour and glitter ultimately faded, revealing the grimmer realities beneath. Still, I emerged wiser and stronger from the experience.

When Michael and I used to go to Piccadilly Station we had an arrangement that at a certain time we would meet at a bar or club in Soho if we weren't busy, and then we'd go home together, but one evening, I met a very nice man called Dennis Sellers. He was a large man with many businesses, such as shirt factories and tech companies, selling things like fax machines, and I ended up moving in with him for a short while because he needed help with day-to-day jobs as he was always so busy.

I stopped escorting for a while at the time but started working in Selfridges doing the window displays and enjoying a bit of interior decorating. I still remember those lovely windows and it was a great creative outlet for me. Then one Saturday, Dennis asked me to help him in his shirt factory. He laid out maybe 50 to 100 layers of cloth, with their templates, and then we put them under the bandsaw and started cutting them out. Ladies would come on the Monday, sew them together and make them into shirts. Dennis also collected English antiques in his house in Ipswich, and he didn't have just any old safe, it was more like a vault! He had expensive glass, silver and even things that belonged to Henry VIII and Queen Victoria! He told me that the collection had been valued at over £3m, and that was back in 1976!

John Neckelmann and me in Monte Carlo 1980 that was a difficult relationship he was an old 49 years, I liked life.

I worked in Bourne and Hollingsworth Oxford Street 1981, there was about 30 staff and I am Farther Christmas

CHAPTER SEVEN: DANGEROUSLY HIGH WINDS!

One Sunday, I was in the William IV and I was a bit drunk, as was the man I was with, an older man of about 35. 'Do you fancy going flying?' He asked me. So, curious to find out what this was all about, I agreed and we jumped into his little sports car and bombed down the road, all the way to Luton.

As promised, we arrived at the aerodrome, and as there were very high winds at the time, I remember an old man cautioning us not to take the plane out as it was too dangerous. But did we listen? No, we did not. We got into the air, where I discovered that the little runway comprised of literally only mud and grass, and we took off! 10 minutes into the flight, however, as if the high winds weren't dangerous enough, my companion announced, 'I'm going to sleep.' Leaving me, at the age of 17, flying the plane for about an hour on my own! I recall trying small manoeuvres, like I'd seen in the movies; turning it a little bit to the left and then to the right, and I tried to take it lower as I knew that if I increased my speed, I would have gone even higher, which I was not too happy about.

Suddenly, over the radio, I heard, 'You're in Heathrow airspace! Leave immediately!' Realising that the gig was up, and being left little choice, I finally elbowed my daredevil friend, who was still fast asleep, and woke him up in the hope that he could get it together just long enough to land the plane! Amazingly, we got home safe and in one piece which was something of a minor miracle!

When I started escorting again, it was in the same place in Piccadilly, and it's worth bearing in mind that these were the days before mobile phones and the internet, so nothing was arranged beforehand. I met a guy in the station one evening called John Neckelmann, a Danish man who imported furniture to England, and he lived in Belsize Park, which is very near Hampstead. We started seeing each other and after a while, I moved in with him. John was 49 and I was 19 by then, so once again there was a large age gap, especially as he was a rather old 49. He'd lived quite a life, smoking and drinking and eating lots of high-cholesterol foods, and he'd already had one heart attack before we met, so his lifestyle must have finally caught up with him.

It turned out that John's family were quite close to the Royal family and that John was very well-educated, and I was pleased at first that he wanted me to help him in his business, although I found it very difficult after a while, because of my dyslexia. I don't speak Danish which didn't help and we developed a very stormy relationship. John liked to stay in, drinking gin and smoking, which I did too, to some extent, but I also wanted to go out, especially as I was only 19!

John would say, 'Go out and have fun!' But when I came back the atmosphere had always turned sour and the shouting and arguing would start. But it wasn't all bad and we did have some good times, including a memorable holiday in Cannes, France, and a few enjoyable trips to Denmark when we drove over from the UK, which was beautiful.

I left John three times in the end however, as things between us were just too stormy, and on the second occasion, I went back to live with Michael, in the flat near Hampstead. Things were fine between Michael and me at first, until he brought another man back to live with us, a man called Mike, who I later discovered was a robber; a cat burglar!

Mike decided he liked me more than Michael and I realised after a while that I had basically become his possession. When he'd been out working in the evening, he would come back full of adrenaline, wanting rough sex and if I said no, he would almost bite my nose off! He drank an awful lot of vodka, which Michael and I started drinking too, but over time, alarm bells really started going off and I knew I had to get out of this situation before something seriously bad happened.

I called my mother and asked her to come and get me, telling her that I'd explain, and thankfully, she did. I didn't speak to Michael for a few weeks and I never spoke to Mike again, but I think he left the flat after a week or two. I moved back in with John, as I didn't think that actually living with my mother was an option, and he promised me that everything would be better, even though, of course, it wasn't.

CHAPTER EIGHT: A MEXICAN ADVENTURE

John had a gold ring made, with his family crest on it, and when I inevitably wanted to leave him for the last time, I gave him back the ring and he gave me £2,000, which I used to go to Mexico on 8th February 1982. I'd met some Mexicans in London when I was working at Bournes & Hollingsworth hairdressers in Oxford Street, and when I'd gone swimming at the YMCA, I'd met Jorge and some of his Mexican friends.

I knew nothing at all about Mexico. I didn't even know it was a Spanish-speaking country, but they'd told me that if I wanted to make some money, I should go to Mexico City; so, I did! My mother went crazy as it was such a long way away, but I used to do that sort of thing back then, even though I had no job, no hotel, just a phone number for Jorge and a head full of optimism.

On the plane, I started talking to a friendly Mexican girl and found out that her father was a diplomat. When we got to the airport her mother was there to meet her and with just a click of her fingers, people parted and our bags were whisked off by a porter, to the family limousine. They took me to their beautiful penthouse, which I was very grateful for, as I was tired from the flight and the fact that the air in Mexico City was thinner than I was used to, but I still needed a hotel. They started to look for places for me, but their price range was in the ballpark of $200/300, whereas mine was more like $20/30, so I didn't see them again after that first night. We were clearly not moving in quite the same circles.

The initial culture shock was intense and the poverty, visible on every corner, was far greater than anything I'd witnessed back in England. On the way to my budget hotel, we drove through neighbourhoods where houses were packed together and children hawked wares at intersections. At the same time, polished diplomats' wives nonchalantly flashed ostentatious jewels as they stepped out of chauffeured cars. I was disturbed by the extreme disparities in wealth.

The city itself overwhelmed my senses. Spanish colonial architecture mingled with sleek modern high-rises. Marimba music drifted from invisible radios as vendors hawked roasted corn and fresh tropical fruit from sidewalk carts. The air was filled with car exhaust and savoury aromas, carried on a warm breeze. My head swam trying to take it all in.

I started to ring the number I had for Jorge, but it took me three days in the end, even though he was only four blocks away as it turned out, in the Zona Rosa (the Pink Zone) which was a bit like Oxford Circus, with lots of interesting shops, restaurants and bars. There were three girls and the two of us staying in the apartment and Jorge was doing some acting work, but tragically, two days after I moved in, he found out that his mother had killed herself.

I gave him some money to go home and see his family, and in exchange, he gave me an address for a part in an advert he had lined up. Jorge had dark skin and brown eyes, whereas I was blonde with green eyes and ridiculously white, but I decided to give it a go anyway. I had to take three suits with me, so I spent hours ironing, and when I got to the place, I could only tell them in English that Jorge's mum had died, but it worked out somehow.

The advert was for TV, for Head and Shoulders, but I just had to walk into an office and appear for a grand total of about four seconds. I did another TV advert after that in Acapulco for Camay soap, and then I even did a photoshoot for a magazine, sitting in a new car in the zoo! This was all great fun, but after I had been in Mexico for about six weeks, I knew that I needed a proper job, and as luck would have it, one of the girls in the flat knew a salon I could apply to.

She'd gone to a party and had started talking to a hairdresser who owned his own salon and luckily, he wanted to employ me, so I called him soon after and over the phone I doubled my income. The salon was extremely posh and very high class, but the owner and his boyfriend were not very nice as it turned out and were a bit dodgy. It was very new and they'd decided to do a TV promotion to raise their profile, so naturally, this advert involved me and a 90-second appearance. But as I had no Spanish at that point, it didn't exactly work out, especially as they weren't even telling me what to do. Luckily, after five weeks, a female manicurist took me to another salon, which was busy but not as posh, and that's where I met Lydia, a Mexican lady who looked a bit like the singer, Dion Warwick, who was 12 years older than me, and who helped to teach me Spanish.

I did not have the right official papers to work in Mexico in those early days and I remember one occasion when men from the council came in looking for me and I had to hide in a cupboard for four hours until the coast was clear! Something had to be done about my work status, so as Lydia and I got on well as friends, we decided to get married, telling no one except the salon owner. Lydia lived with her mother, sister and her dad but we brought some of her clothes over to my place to make it look like she lived there with me. She'd had a hard life so we were both supportive of each other at the time, and I knew that Lydia's background was very sad. She'd had polio when she was small which had left her with a limp, and her mother – a Mexican Indian from the mountains – had told her that no man would want her because of it and that men were bad anyway, so she was lucky. Lydia's mum didn't have any shoes until she was 20, and her dad was a drunk.

Unsurprisingly, Lydia's upbringing had caused a number of mental health problems and she would sometimes drink a lot and get very drunk. At my flat one night, I was in bed fast asleep when she came into the room and jumped on me, trying to have sex! She still had her tights on, thank God, but in the morning, she didn't even remember it happening. Around this time, my mum, Mum's new husband, Don, and Carol actually came to visit me in Mexico, in 1983, and we went to see the pyramids and did a bit of sightseeing. While we were walking around the pyramids, however, I saw something shiny in this lump of mud, and it turned out to be a white gold ring with 32 diamonds in it! I still have some of the diamonds, but over the years they've been added to different presents for people.

Meanwhile, back at the salon, I found out that one of my clients was part of the Wrigley's Spearmint family but unfortunately, the only guy I dated in the three years I was there was a penniless taxi driver called John, with a very old and dangerous taxi (although he was really nice and it lasted about six months).

Near the end of my stay, Lydia and I put our money together and opened a salon of our own, but I had to make sure all my papers were absolutely perfect as they would've got me kicked out of the country if they wanted. The Mexican authorities weren't happy with me opening my own shop. But Lydia and I painted the walls and employed some workmen to do things up for us. It looked good and after a while we were fortunate enough to get some very rich clients, covered with diamonds, and ready to splash the cash, although it was hard work, speaking Spanish all day, and looking after the staff and the clients with Lydia.

I needed a holiday and wanted to go back home after a while, so I packed my bags, got my papers together and headed for the airport. Unfortunately, when I got to the check-in desk, a policeman asked me for my national service papers. 'I'm a foreign national.' I told him, but he replied, 'If you become Mexican before you're 25, you have to do national service.' With machine guns in hand, they then took me to the plane to get my bags and I then had to return to the flat.

I had to go to this enormous football stadium full of 3,000 or even 4,000 young boys and I was the oldest one there. A colonel with a microphone was taking one black ball or one white ball out of a bag and then saying people's names, and if you got a black ball you didn't have to do the National Service. I had to go downstairs to read my name because I couldn't understand a word he was saying, but when I found it, it said, black ball, which thankfully meant I didn't have to do it after all!

'I have to get back to England,' I told Lydia in a panic, but in the end, as Mexico was quite corrupt, it took about eight months to buy my way out and get a divorce. In 1982, the exchange rate went from 25 pesos to 2000 for one dollar, in 1985. So at the end of it all, I left with about the same amount of money I'd started off with – about £2,000.

1982 just before I went to Mexico. Photo for modelling, I didn't do modelling but 3 adverts for TV and a magazine.

Mexico 1984 John was my boyfriend and Lydia my wife and me.

Lydia (ex-wife) and me in Paris 1987

May 17, 2011

We went on a cruise 2011 Mum and Step Father Don they both have now passed away.
XXXX they came to Mexico to visit

CHAPTER NINE: HOME SWEET HOME AND A NEW SALON

When I came back from Mexico in January 1985, I moved in with my mother and Don for a while. I had actually been to their wedding in 1979, but by now they'd moved to Shepperton, in Middlesex, where I slept in the small bedroom at the front. I started doing mobile hairdressing and got busy quite quickly, but as anticipated, living with my mother and stepfather wasn't easy.

I got a dog called Jason, who was just about to be put down; a very sweet dog and very intelligent, so it made me feel good to know that I had played a part in making sure he was happy and safe, and he did give me a little bit of company at home. Mum and Don used to go to bed at 9 p.m., maybe 8:45, but I wouldn't get back from hairdressing until about 10, and as it was a bungalow, I always had to creep in and tiptoe around. At the time, I remember being desperate to see the Live Aid concert that everyone was talking about that year, but as Don didn't like any kind of music whatsoever, neither bongo drums nor opera, I had to watch it on a black and white television set in the garage. It was one of the hottest days of the year, so needless to say, I was not amused.

There were other things which just didn't feel right about living with Mum and Don, so after a while, I decided to purchase a mobile home, with the help of a bank loan. It was a good place, with a lovely garden, it felt very friendly and safe, and I got quite a lot of clients coming to the site. I was there for about 18 months before I decided to open a salon, and I was lucky enough to find one in Datchet, in 1988, next to Windsor. The mobile home cost me £12,000, but I sold it for £22,000, so that was some very good news.

I'll always remember one of my customers at that salon telling us that Windsor Castle was on fire. 'Don't be silly,' we told her. But sure enough, when we went out into the garden to look, it was true. It looked like a huge sunset, but it was actually quite beautiful, but also incredibly sad.

When Diana died, I'd never known a village to go so quiet, and I had people cancelling their appointments for weeks because they were in mourning and they just couldn't cope with going outside. It was quite remarkable.

I had fun painting the salon, in a mix of grey and pink, and I proudly decided to call it David Lloyd. It had been something of an old person's salon, so it already had some regular clientele. As you can imagine, they required a lot of sets, perms and blow-dries, all the things that people don't generally do these days, although I don't understand why as they're big money makers.

I had that salon for eight years and it was in a very good area for spotting celebrities of the day. Over the years, I saw the Queen, the Queen Mother, Elton John and even Russian President, Mikhail Gorbachev. I even bumped into Princess Diana once outside the shop before her passing.

My salon in Datchet from 1988 to 1996, I had some lovely clients and staff, I lived up stairs for 4 years.

First time I went out unisex 1990 Rocky Horror in a pub in Windsor.

One Christmas in Datchet, me as Fred Flintstone yes its my beard. We always dressed up for Christmas. Great fun thanks X

CHAPTER TEN: LIFE WITH KEITH AND A CHANCE ENCOUNTER

The second year I was in Datchet, I met someone called Keith, a civil servant, and he became a big part of my life as we were together for nine years. He was very kind, very soft and we lived above the shop before we could actually buy a house in Hersham; an old Edwardian house, which we filled with antiques. I made the curtains and we enjoyed making it cosy and homely. My dog, Jason, was with us for a while, until he became ill, but we also bought three chihuahuas and a Great Dane.

I've always found it difficult to say no – like the relationship I had with Keith – and I look back now and wonder whether we should ever really have got together. He was a lovely person and easy to get on with, but it was difficult too at times. The first time we were in bed, we were like two women. We didn't know what to do! Somehow, however, we decided to have a proper relationship, although I remember taking the dogs out for a very long walk over Windsor Great Park and having a big conversation with myself. When I came back, I decided I was going to be 'the man' in the bedroom. I talked myself into it.

The salon was doing quite well, but it was still stressful, like any other business, although I had some wonderful clients there. One was called Mrs Piggott, a music teacher and a very,

very lovely lady. She used to write her cheques once a week with a fountain pen, with the most beautiful handwriting you had ever seen. She's passed away now, sadly.

Keith and I went on holiday to Brighton with our three chihuahuas and our Great Dane on one occasion, and while we were away, we couldn't resist going to this enormous antiques fair. We were just about to leave when we decided to walk a little more around this huge building that looked like an aeroplane hangar when I suddenly noticed a slightly chubby man, sitting there, rolling a cigarette. It was my old friend, Michael.

We had lost contact for 14 years, maybe longer, but there he was, and when he looked up at me, it was as if 14 years had never passed by. We exchanged phone numbers and I found out that the love of his life, Stephen, was still alive but extremely ill with AIDS. It was quite strange. Michael had met Stephen just before I'd gone to Mexico, about three months before, but after my return, I only got to know him for just a few months before he died. It was as if I was only destined to see the beginning and the end of their relationship and nothing in between in all those years. I've always thought this was strange as if I was not supposed to be in their life when they were together.

Stephen was a lovely guy, 6 foot 4" and built like a brick house, but soft in nature. He was a builder, a carpenter, a plumber – he did everything. But then I went to Mexico and Michael and I lost touch. Stephen was Michael's soulmate and it really hurt him when he died in 1996. I think it almost destroyed him. Stephen died in his arms…

BLOOD, SWEAT AND SUSPENDERS

As for me, Keith's drinking had increased, which was really starting to wear me down, especially as he had a bad habit of nearly always passing out at parties. I found this really embarrassing, so in the end, I decided enough was enough and we sold the house. I had to rehome the dogs, which broke my heart a little as they were my children, but I knew I couldn't look after them as I needed to work.

In 1997, Michael and I went to Toronto, Canada, as he needed to get away after Stephen died, and we had a lovely time. We were away for 10 days. We hired a motorhome and drove 1,800 miles. Michael did the map reading, I did the driving and it was great fun. I nearly trod on a snake, in just my flip-flops, but I lived to tell the tale and we had a great time, seeing a moose, chipmunks, squirrels and a huge assortment of different birds. The weather was incredible too, at the end of April/beginning of May and we made some wonderful memories.

Keith my partner for 9 years 1994 he was very lovely.

This is Mike and Steve, Michael was my best friend for over 30 years. Steve was his love he died in 1996 xxx

CHAPTER ELEVEN: MOPS, MOWERS AND A REVOLUTIONARY IDEA

I sold the salon in 1996 and started up a company called Mops and Mowers, a gardening company. The mops were for house cleaning in the winter and the mowers were obviously for gardening. It was general maintenance, basically, and I thoroughly enjoyed it. All the old lady customers used to give me a cup of tea and biscuits and some of them actually wanted me to do their hair as well. I used to do their gardens and then do their hair!

I nearly got to do Prince Andrew and Fergie's garden once but they started to argue, and the Queen didn't buy them the house. I don't think they pay their bills very quickly, so I didn't mind, but their estate was huge; many, many acres. I would have had to have given up all my other customers so it was probably for the best and I'm glad now that I didn't get the job, but it was an interesting proposition.

As usual, I was extremely busy and working 14-hour days, but I loved the work, even though it was very hard at times. One major advantage was that I'd never been so fit in my life and it also helped that I was able to call on people I knew if someone wanted a wall or a pond building. Michael was managing an antique business, which was ticking over, but I don't think he ever made any large sums of money. The gardening wasn't going to make me rich either, even though I was very busy, so, I can't remember who suggested it, but I started doing escort work again in my local area.

I remember this guy turning up at my flat, who also came again a few weeks later, but one day, he suddenly looked a bit shocked. 'What is it?' I asked him, confused, and he told me that he'd seen a photograph of my mother who lived next door but one from him, which I found rather amusing.

Eventually, I sold the business in 1999, as well as my flat and moved in with Michael, in Hoddesdon. Michael was still doing antiques and I was helping him by this time, but I had some money in the bank from the sale of the flat; not a huge amount, but enough for a while.

We had some really lovely Christmases in Hoddesdon and the garden there was very overgrown, full of ivy and holly. Michael used to invite his friends round for drinks and lots of smokes and we used to make garlands and wreaths and put the tree up. It was great, and when I remember those days, they still make me smile. I really did like those Christmases, and he had the most beautiful Victorian tree and decorations.

We started doing a bit more escort work and it ticked over, although not very well to be honest, as it soon seemed that gay men now wanted great big hunky, hairy men, which did not describe the two of us.

'Where to look?' I thought, so as there was now a rudimentary form of the internet, I searched online and in the papers looking for ways to make more money from the escorting. Doing male escorting in Hoddesdon was not going very well after a while, so eventually I found a brothel in Hounslow, which was quite a journey, and I ended up taking a room in this house, which had an Asian girl working there, who was extremely busy.

Myself and occasionally some other girls worked there as well, but I soon discovered that I was actually spending more money than I was making, due to paying for fuel for the van. I was getting a bit panicked, wondering what I was going to do next when I got talking to the maid, Joan, who looked like she ate concrete for breakfast, and you would not have wanted to mess with her! She's very, very important in this story, however, because without her my other life would not have started. We were sitting together in the front room when she said, 'Why don't you do what my friend does?'

'What's that?' I asked her.

'He puts on some makeup, as well as a wig and a dress and calls himself Paula. Once he's made £300 in a day, he stops working! Go home,' she said, 'put a wig on, some makeup and a dress and then put an advert in the paper saying TV (transvestite) escort.'

I wasn't making £300 in a month, so you know what I did? Of course, you do… I got in the van, went back to Michael and said, 'This is what we're doing.' He wasn't quite sure and said no at first, but in the end, we did it. We went out shopping for all our paraphernalia, thinking we were going to look gorgeous, and we even put adverts in the local newspaper with our mobile numbers. We had two ads, one for me, and one for him, and the phones went berserk! We couldn't answer quickly enough!

1997 first party dressed

Me not quite got it right. 1999 well if I can myself looking better anyone can. Gorgeous XX

CHAPTER TWELVE: TIFFANY AND JANE CARRY ON AGAIN

Every time we went out shopping with the phones, they were melting in our pockets. It was insane. We thought people were taking the piss at first until they all started actually turning up. They came to us, we never went to them, and one day I even remember being upstairs with this old man who turned up looking like the Queen Mother. He had a little grey wig, pearls, earrings and a tweed suit. 'What am I going to do with this?' I wondered, but then he suddenly had a funny turn.

'Thank God. There is a God,' I thought as I went downstairs and showed him out.

I looked into the living room and saw lots of other men, with Michael dressed up as Jane, right in the middle of them. 'Who are all those men waiting for?' I asked him and he told me that they were all there for me! There were eight of them just sitting expectantly in the living room, but we've learnt since that you never let clients meet each other; it's just not done (although we didn't know that at the time). The last one was sitting there for maybe three hours or more, waiting for me, but that's never happened before or since.

It was all hilarious, to be honest, and such great fun, but we moved from Hoddesdon to a maisonette in Bromley by Bow, which we bought for £55,000, and 18 months later, was valued at £127,000! We were always very busy and even more so when we decided to set up a dressing agency, where guys could come and try on different outfits. We even offered a fantasy day, but that was a lot of hard work to organise.

In 2000, I met a guy called Steven, a pursuit driver for the police. He was lovely, with blonde hair and blue eyes and he used to drive past the flat in Bromley by Bow two or three times a day and pop in for a cup of tea. I met him through a friend called Blossom when my first computer went wrong and she'd said, 'I know someone who could mend it.' And that was Steven, who had knocked on my door when I'd just got out of the bath. At the time I had long blonde extensions in my hair and I opened the door with a towel around me. Apparently, when Steven saw me, he fell in love immediately.

We didn't have sex all the time as he used to like just being with me and talking. The strange thing is, however, that every time he turned up, I could guarantee I would become busy. He was almost like a lucky rabbit's foot! Most of the time Steven spent his time spent talking to Michael while I was upstairs working. We saw each other for about nine months, although he was married with two children…

I was always busier than Jane, perhaps because I was blonde, and Jane was dark-haired. But we both had all sorts of different clients and I went by the name of Tiffany, in homage to the old *Carry On* films I loved, films like *Carry On Up the Khyber*, where they make jokes about 'a bit of Tiffin' and other silly but entertaining inuendoes.

My first customers tended to be builders, tradesmen and other working-class blokes around my age. I had imagined most clients would be creepy old perverts or office drones, but the majority were just regular men who didn't have the courage or opportunity to explore their hidden fantasies until Tiffany came along. They found me approachable and non-judgemental, which put them at ease. I quickly grew confident in my new role, learning how to put clients at ease while still screening out any sketchy characters or time wasters. Turning down the men who gave off bad vibes was an essential skill to stay safe. Thankfully, I had a keen intuition for filtering genuine customers from trouble.

To my surprise, I enjoyed escorting far more than hairdressing. I was still shy at heart, but showing up as Tiffany gave me a thrilling new identity. My clients respected and desired me, which did wonders for my self-esteem. After a childhood spent ignored by my self-absorbed parents and mocked by school bullies for my perceived effeminacy, it felt amazing to be appreciated exactly as I was. No longer did I need to hide my playful, flamboyant personality. And I was earning more from a few evenings escorting than an entire week styling hair! Why had I waited so long to advertise my true self?

We had a lot of builders and I remember one guy who turned up and wanted to dress in the full shebang: wig, makeup, frocks, high heels, the lot. He spoke just like an East End gangster, which I think he might well have been, and every so often he had to take a call on his mobile, to talk to his driver: 'Yes, mate.' He'd say, 'I'm still in the meeting but I'll be with you shortly.' When in actual fact, there he was on the bed with a skirt up around his waist. I think if his driver had seen him, he might have been shot…

Around this time, Channel 4 decided that they wanted to do a programme about transexual escorts, which I was involved in the making of, although Michael didn't want to take part. I couldn't get an actual customer to participate, unfortunately, so in the end, the guy from Channel 4 had to pretend to be in the cast. He knocked on the door, I opened it, let him in, and then the camera just filmed us going upstairs. I never saw it on television, so I'm not even sure it was ever released, and I didn't make any money, but it had been interesting doing the interviews and talking about our work. It's quite interesting... I can tell people who watch a lot of porn because of how they re-act. How they have sex is usually with no rhythm, just a lot of effort, which is not always that enjoyable..!

Michael (Jane) and me in Thailand 2000 just before we opened Stunners

This is Thailand 2000 he made me some wonderful clothes.

This was for channel 4, filming me for the show, The Clinic. 2001. I had a facelift and they filmed it. I have a copy.

CHAPTER THIRTEEN: ABSOLUTE STUNNERS

There was a nightclub that Michael and I used to go to back then called Ron Stormes, in Stepney, East London, and it was a lovely club, really friendly. It was literally a meet and greet and a place to dance and I loved the way the dance floor used to light up like we were in the '70s. We used to go there every Saturday along with another popular club of the time called The WayOut, in Limehouse, which is still open as far as I know, although Ron Storme died back in 2001.

Michael and I started talking about the possibility of opening another club around this time and when the idea was finally a reality, we decided to call it Stunners, as we had often been referred to as such by our clients. It was on Kingsland Road, just up from Liverpool Street Station, under the railway arch, and typically for Michael and I, we decided to do things slightly differently.

We had quite a lot of different people working for us and quite a big turnover of staff, and one of them was called Ritzi Crackers. He was (or she is) an extraordinary person – very artistic and full of wonderful ideas. With a piece of cotton, a bit of netting and some curtains she could make you an outfit, and she'd been doing drag all over London, and working in Madame Jojo's for quite a few years. She even had her own slot doing her own show, and I think she was only 17 or 18 when she started at our club. She would walk around with a ball whip cracking it in the air, although we had to stop her in the end as it was dangerous (though a lot of fun!).

It was enormous inside and had wonderful exposed brickwork which gave it an earthy feel, and we had a dungeon, dark rooms, video rooms, a harem room and lots of curtains, pillows and cushions strewn around the place for maximum comfort. We had a large dancefloor, a nice bar and the entrance was like a cinema, where you came in through the big, fancy doors and paid at the little booth, just like people used to do at the old movie theatres; then the double doors would lead into the nightclub.

It didn't start off very busy, but within a few months, we had over 250 people in there, which took us by surprise. We ran out of everything the first weekend, so we had to run to the local shops and buy everything they had, but we didn't pay for the electricity or water. We didn't have all the official licences, so you could say it was a bit of an underground club, but it was a lot of fun. The clientele included judges, rocket scientists, policemen and yet again, lots of builders. It was aimed mainly at transexuals and gay men, that was the point of the club, but of course, there were people there who'd just come out of curiosity and a little bit of 'how's yer father.'

I was still a transvestite when we first opened Stunners, but I started growing my hair, as I hated wearing wigs anyway, and I got a boob job in 2001/2 when I became transexual and I chose the name, Andrea. In the hedonistic embrace of Stunners, I finally felt free to take the leap, and with

Michael's support, I began transitioning fully to the woman I knew myself to be inside. I was reborn and it was glorious!

Owning and managing Stunners kept me busy as a queen bee, but I still found time for the final phase in my transition – changing all my legal documentation. My solicitors smoothly handled the paperwork converting the 'M' on my passport and driver's license to an 'F', and the metamorphosis was complete! My close friends threw a tremendously touching graduation party to welcome Andrea to the world, and I wept tears of happiness on seeing 'Andrea Orme' for the first time spelt out on those official cards and papers. It was utterly life-affirming.

This was mine and Jane's trans and gay sex club. 2001 to 2013, Stunners.

Me in the dungeon at stunners 2002.

Ritzy great person very artistic she was 17 years old when she joined us in Stunners. Walking around with a whip.

Dawn and me, 2002 Halloween. She worked in a funeral parlour and was an escort.

CHAPTER FOURTEEN: PHIL'S A TWAT

One morning, things started to take a turn for the worse, when I came down to breakfast in the maisonette – this was in 2001 – and there was a guy in the kitchen with a cowboy hat on, by the name of Phil. He turned out to be the biggest twat ever but he was now in a relationship with Michael, although I think Michael only liked him because he had a big willy.

The problem was that he and his big willy never seemed to go away. He came to the club regularly and even started getting involved in the day-to-day running of things, as well as bringing people back after the club was closed. I never used drink or drugs as I had to drive them home, so when I was trying to get to sleep, I had to put up with a lot of loud talking, laughing, slamming doors and flushing toilets, and by the time they eventually went to sleep, I was getting up, and the living room was full of naked people!

Before long I'd had enough – I had to get my own place to get away from Phil and all his drug-crazy friends who stayed over the whole weekends – so I bought myself another maisonette, in Bow. I went to see it in stilettos and a mink coat, and although it had been burnt out, everything was new; the floors, the walls, everything. There were builders on their hands and knees laying flooring whilst I walked around them like Miss Whiplash; nevertheless, I said to the agent, 'I'll have it, thank you,' and that was that, for a mere £120,000: three large double bedrooms upstairs, a single bedroom, a shower room with a basin, a bathroom with a power shower and bath. And downstairs a dining room, living room (with no naked people), a kitchen and downstairs toilet. To top it off, it had a lovely front garden and a back garden as well.

Life was good and the club was busy, but then we found out that Phil was taking money from the tills, as well as trying to pull rank over major business decisions. Soon Phil wormed his way into helping manage Stunners, though his only talent was skimming from the till and tricking Michael into covering his unpaid bar tabs. The oily creep resented my authority, trying at every turn to undermine me and assume control. It wasn't long before our philosophical differences over the club's direction led to explosive fights that left the whole staff trembling. We had a staff meeting and he stood up to speak, but I'd had enough by that point, and although I'm usually a fairly calm person, I do have a temper and it came out full force, in his direction! The stress started affecting my performance until I finally realised I needed a break before I had a full mental collapse. Leaving my beloved Stunners in Michael's incapable hands was devastating, but I had no choice, and of course, Phil eagerly swooped in to claim my place. I ended up leaving the club as I could not listen to his shit for another second and that was the end of that – all thanks to Phil and his stupid big willy.

Though it broke my heart to abandon my crew and players, I consoled myself that this was but a temporary respite to recover my strength and firmness of purpose. Once revived, I would reclaim my rightful place and oust the scoundrel trying to steal all I'd worked for.

With my come and get me clothes on after losing my club.

CHAPTER FIFTEEN: DARK DAYS IN CAMBRIDGE

In 2002, there was a bit of good news, as I had a facelift which was filmed for the Channel 4 programme *The Clinic*. I continued escorting from my flat but also had some TV work, so the money was streaming in. They were good times, but it got so busy that I had to close for a day or two, so the neighbours didn't see too many men coming in! There was one black guy I remember who was always high and went outside once to get something he'd forgotten from his car, completely naked! You can just imagine the curtain twitchers, as this 6 foot 3" black man wandered out of my place in the nude in the middle of the day; although I don't think anyone saw him.

I got friendly with a girl called Dawn at this point, who lived in Cambridge, and I used to go to her flat where we worked together a few times. I don't do women but we worked on the same guy and it worked out OK, so I decided, in 2003, to move to Cambridge on a long-term basis, leaving Michael to find some friends to rent my maisonette. I don't know why I moved to Cambridge when I look back on it now; that is a regret, although I bought a two-bedroom house, so at least I now have a 50% share in two large maisonettes in London and my own house in Cambridge.

I carried on working from Dawn's flat and a bit from my house, but after a while, I decided to open a hairdressing salon, this time with a carwash at the back. To do this, I decided to change from Andrea back to David, which meant having my boobs removed, but I felt at the time that it would help the business. The carwash consisted of three young male employees and two high-pressure sprays, with the front of the building being used as an office, which I then turned into a rather large salon.

We had a reception room and two other rooms, giving us enough space for four stylists, and I employed a few new people. Unfortunately, they weren't like the staff I'd employed before as they didn't seem to care about their work as much (although they dutifully got on with it nevertheless). The carwash didn't do as well as I thought, so I closed that down eventually as I couldn't pay the boys, but by then Michael needed to sell the house as the London club wasn't doing very well either.

As the salon was also struggling, I decided to take the carwash away and turn it into a beauty salon, for which I used £100,000 to build the beautician's area and pay off some bills. Things still weren't working very well sadly, even after those investments, and regretfully I had to start using credit cards. At the end of it all, I'd used the £100,000 in cash plus £84,000 in credit cards which resulted in bankruptcy.

Before this happened, however, I'd received a letter in the post asking if I needed help with employment law, regarding my staff. I actually threw it in the bin at first but for some reason, I changed my mind and decided to call the lady's number. The lady at the end of the phone was called Jayne and she came over to my house where we had a chat about the laws as she was an HR specialist.

She actually invited me round to her house for Christmas in the end as we'd got on so well, and as I was still struggling with the mortgage due to the decline in the success of the salon, Jayne started living at mine for a while. She'd seen me on TV having a facelift, even though I was Andrea then and now I was David, so she knew a bit about my life. We worked with Herbalife after I had to get rid of the salon – a dietary company which helps you stay slim and fit – but it was very hard work and we made no money. We spent more money than we made going to all the different shows they had in Spain, France and Germany. Some people who'd been at it for years had some luck and were making from £10,000, even up to £100,000 a month, but it was a pyramid scheme essentially, and we ended up broke.

It was a shame, but over time it became clear that she wanted more than just friendship, and there was also the issue of her three children, one of whom was a nasty piece of work called Chris. He ended up stealing money from me and his mum; we had to bail him out of prison on one occasion, and we even had to buy him a car that he then wrote off in Greece. He was a monster.

Needless to say, life was not going very well at this point, what with me not having any money, then losing the salon and going bankrupt and Jayne's children coming over to the house at all hours of the day and night. Things started to get very dark indeed…

I reached a really low point one morning, after I'd said goodbye to Jayne as she left for work. I went to the shops, got a bottle of wine and a great big bottle of paracetamol, and then back at home, I immediately started to drink all the alcohol and downed loads and loads of pills. I even said goodbye to my dog, Benji, my little Chihuahua.

I woke up in the hospital, so I'd been pulled back from the brink, but that was not a good feeling. The failure of having to see the faces that I didn't want to see again, and then having to talk about it made me shudder. The nurses insisted that whilst I was in the hospital I saw a psychiatrist, which I did and luckily, I found a really nice lady who helped me hugely. I have to say, through her, I managed to leave Cambridge, Jayne and my house. I actually ended up leaving in a small van with just the van keys and as much furniture as it would hold.

And that was all I had. By now, it was 2008 and I had no job, no house, nothing, just my dear little Chihuahua and some furniture. I started to drive down the motorway towards London, honestly not knowing what to do, but I decided to call Michael. We'd stayed in touch, although not on a regular basis, and when I told him what I was doing, he let me stay. 'I don't know what we're going to do with your furniture, but we'll sort it,' he told me, which was a big relief, although there was still one big problem: Phil and his big, bloody willy...

Me and Jayne she moved in with me! 2005 I had gone back to being male :(

I do not recognise me, but it was dark days. Everything was going wrong, business and life.

My salon in Bar Hill, Cambridge with car wash and beauty salon. I lost 3 houses 100,000 cash and 84,000 in credit cards

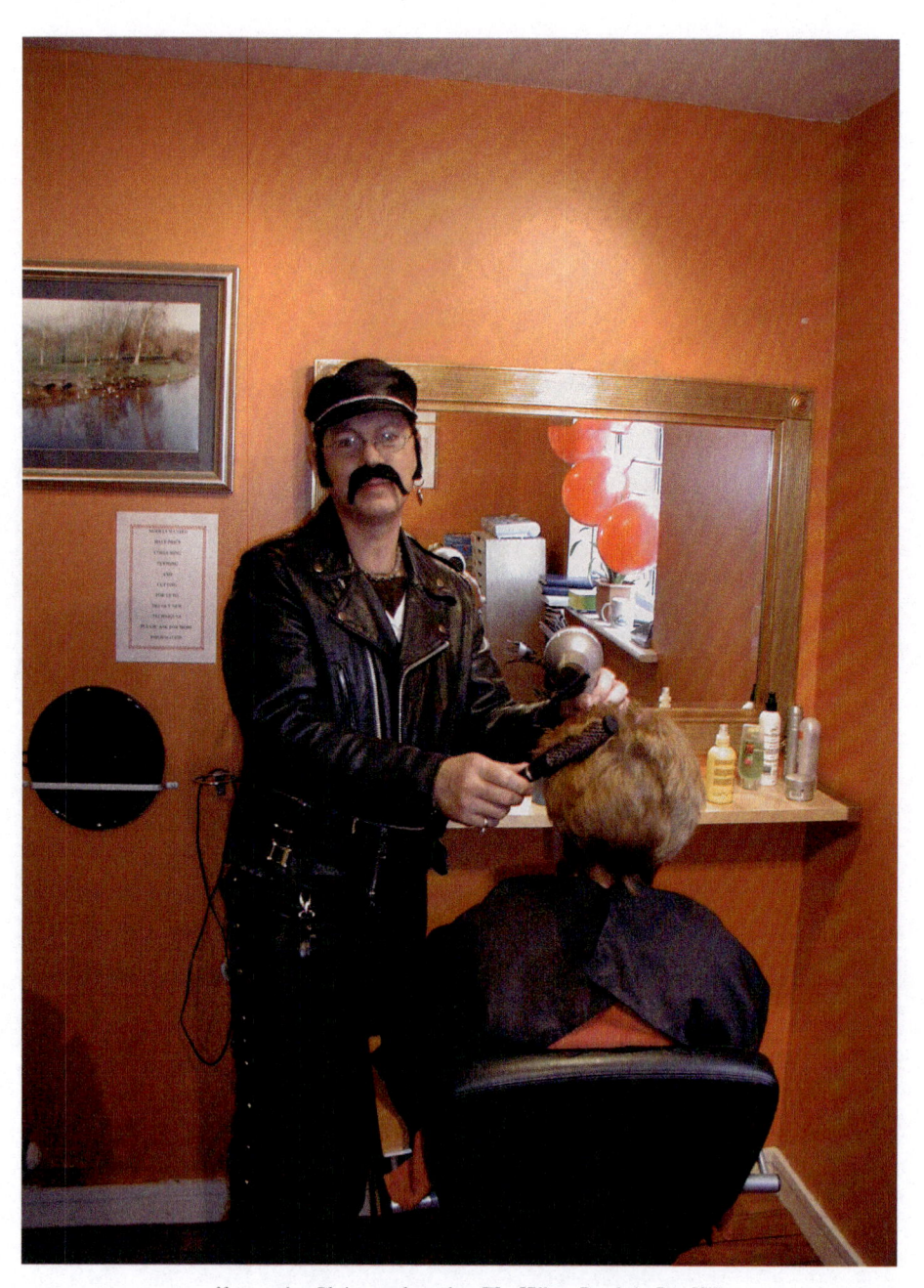

Yes, another Christmas dressed as The Village People in Bar Hill.

CHAPTER SIXTEEN: LIFE WITH BLOSSOM WAS NOT BLOSSOMING

That twat, Phil, was still with Michael, so as there was no bedroom for me to sleep in, I had to resort to sleeping in my leather chair with my Chihuahua, Benji. I lived in that chair, and unfortunately, Michael was heavily into drugs by now; all sorts of different drugs. The club, Stunners, was still up and running so I went there and helped out, working behind the bar and taking the money, but I got in touch with my friend Blossom; a man, but a man with a bosom, which 'she' had put in because she liked black men and black men like bosoms. Her actual name was John, but she used the name Blossom as well as Carol, her escorting name and the name she used for his cabaret and drag shows. Blossom was her everyday name and John was the name she used if she had to do something official.

I went round to see her but her flat was in a terrible state as she was quite a lot older than me and was suffering from Alzheimer's. I started escorting from there because Blossom used to do it too, although not at that same time. She had a bedroom to let so I moved in, which meant I had my own room and a small little sitting room upstairs. It was much better than the chair at Michael's, although Blossom was an extreme hoarder, and her home was utterly filthy. Piles of trash covered every surface and the kitchen swarmed with roaches and stank of rot. Blossom never cleaned and refused to hire help, but worst of all was the spare bedroom where she kept her un-housebroken dogs, and the carpet was saturated with years of urine and faeces. The stench could make your eyes water!

So, I started making some money - with my boobs put back in at this point - but Blossom was not the easiest person to live with by any means, and we fell out because I used to come home at seven in the morning, back from the club on a Sunday, and at 11 she'd come into the bedroom and say, 'Come on! Let's get up and go to Lidl!'

One morning we were driving there and I just said, 'I can't do this anymore. It's driving me mad!' She got really angry and we went home, where she proceeded not to speak to me for a week. As a consequence of all this, I ended up moving into an apartment round the corner, in another road, where I stayed for about 18 months until the apartment next to Blossom's came up for rent, and I moved in there. It was a three-bedroom flat next door! She was number 70 and mine was 72.

I was thrilled to reclaim my independence, although I continued being Blossom's friend and carer for eight years after that, doing jobs for her, running errands, escorting at the same time, and working in the club.

Blossom had fingers in quite a lot of pies and she was head of the Glamis estate, which was where I was living in Shadwell. We went to Westminster one day, where Boris

Johnson (who was then Major of London) was giving out certificates for all sorts of different things. 'Why not..!' I thought, as I slowly edged my way towards him and slung my arm around his waist whilst a friend took a photo! I have used the photo on my Facebook account with a comment saying, 'the engagement will be announced shortly.' I was never told to take it down...

The club was in Limehouse now, but it was a good venue, and large. It was quite busy; not every week or every day, but it was ticking over, although it was being run badly because of that twat, Phil, who was still stealing money from the tills by the handful! Michael just didn't know what to do. Most of the time he seemed to be off his head, on something, but I think he'd basically just given up on life by that point. He ended up living in one of the offices and didn't even bother going home anymore.

I came back from Cambridge and started again, not had my boobs put back in yet.
Ascot 2009

A new look I was trying out, Queens Jubilee. 2010

I Met Boris the Mayor of London at a meeting in Westminster briefly.

CHAPTER SEVENTEEN: A FABULOUSLY SAD SEND-OFF

I'd been around, helping out for five years after I came back to London, and then suddenly, one day in 2013, I was told that Michael had died in Ritzi Cracker's flat. It was an enormous shock to me after 30 years of knowing him and I put it out on Facebook thousands of times to let all the customers know that Jane/Michael had passed; there was not a word from my family, not a single word, and they were all on Facebook.

Michael died in May, which was the same month as my mother's birthday, and as she was going around to my sister's for a meal, I asked her if she would make sure that she let Carol know about Michael's death. The next day I called my mother and she said, 'Yes, I mentioned it,' so I waited another day for my sister's response but nothing happened. I have to say, I was very, very angry and in the end, the best they could come up with was, 'We didn't like him.'

You don't say sorry for the person who's dead… you say sorry for the person who's left behind, so it didn't really say a lot for my family. I have to say, I have never forgiven them for that. I do speak to my sister occasionally, but as for my nieces, I don't really speak to them. They've not invited me to their weddings or christenings or anything like that.

BLOOD, SWEAT AND SUSPENDERS

The police took Michael's phone after he died, and I kept on asking for it back so I could get hold of his sister, but they kept saying it was in a cupboard and they didn't have the key. That went on for three weeks and then I found out that the head of police was having a meeting at the local council office, so I phoned the station in Limehouse, saying, 'If I don't get it by tomorrow, I'm going to the meeting and I will make such a noise!' Funnily enough, 20 minutes later they said, 'We've got the key. Come and get your phone.'

I got hold of his sister, who lived in Derby, I believe. I had met her once, many, many, many years ago, but this time I had to tell her that Michael had passed away, and within the first 5 minutes, she said, 'I've got no money.' 'Don't worry.' I replied. 'I will pay for everything.'

We had a very big bash at Stunners to raise the money for Michael's funeral and we even had black horses and a black carriage; a proper East End funeral. He would have loved it and I have to say, it was wonderful. I'd invited all the customers who wanted to come, with no obligation, but lots of people came. Some arrived straight from work, in posh suits and dresses, but many of them came as their fantasy selves, in gothic makeup and hair, with long nails, stilettos and thigh-length boots. There was standing room only left, with half of them outside! For the big bash we wanted we needed money, so I stopped Phil coming to the club as he wasn't the most popular person amongst Michael's friends, although I did say he could come to the Funeral, but he never turned up in the end.

After the funeral, we went to the club, which was still open, and we had lots of drinks, some food, and I have to say, some substances which you can only get from certain people. I'll leave that up to you to imagine, but there was a lot of it, and the next day, the club had to close because the landlord insisted. I carried on escorting in my three-bedroom apartment however, and the clients ranged from policemen to murderers, loads of builders, two cage fighters – one black, one white – and a few firemen for good measure.

I think men find me easy to get on with because I know what I'm doing. I'm not overly dominant but I do take over. I do ask what they do for a living to make it a little bit more personal, and sometimes they say things that are really interesting, and sometimes not. If they say, 'I only work in a warehouse', or, 'I only work in an office.' I'll say, 'Well, someone has to, honey!'

Most clients were fine and I was good at screening out the dodgy ones, but I do remember one Asian guy in a turban who turned up and things went very badly. I had seen him once before and he was only small and seemed pretty harmless, but this time I could tell he'd been sniffing something and he went psychotic! He started running around, looking in cupboards and drawers and even behind the doors as he was convinced that people were hiding there. He then took the keys out of my front door and wouldn't give them back.

I realised there were two options open to me: I could have got extremely angry, picked him up and thrown him over the balcony, which I thought was perhaps not a good idea, and the other way was to stay quiet and keep control of myself. I chose option two, but it took 12 hours to get him out of the flat in the end! Even the murderers were easier than that guy. I asked one of them once, 'What have you been up to?' And the reply was, '15 years for murder.' But it didn't worry me. I decided that they would have no reason to murder little old me and I was usually very good at reading people. You don't always get it right, but you do get better at it and you can usually feel the vibes if someone's good or dangerously weird. There was another guy, who I wouldn't say was dangerously weird, but he was certainly weird. He had one eye missing and he actually asked me to put my appendage in his eye socket, which I did! Strange but true!

If I had one piece of advice for young people today considering escort work, it would be not to compromise your comfort or safety for any amount of money. At first, you may agree to acts or appointments that leave you uneasy just because the money seems too good to pass up. I made that mistake a few times myself! But take it from me, no cash payment is worth feeling violated or endangered. Don't be afraid to walk out on a client who ignores your boundaries. Over time and with experience, you will learn to recognise the gentlemen worth your time. But stay vigilant against letting desperation or greed cloud your judgement.

I don't make customers my friends because I only have sex with strangers. If someone becomes a friend, it gets weird and I just can't have sex with that person. It is a big problem of mine and it may be because of all the abuse that I've endured over the years. I really don't know…

CHAPTER EIGHTEEN: THE PINK BOA AND A PSYCHOPATH, LYING PIECE OF RUBBISH

After Michael died, people kept saying to me, 'Open another club!' But the club had basically died with Michael and the landlord wanted the property back. I just couldn't be bothered back then, and I needed time as Michael's death had hurt me deeply. However, about a year later, I decided to open up the very first transexual lap-dancing club in Europe, called The Pink Boa. In the vibrant heart of London's East End, amidst the eclectic tapestry of culture and nightlife, it emerged as a groundbreaking establishment that I hoped would redefine the boundaries of entertainment.

Nestled in the heart of the bustling metropolis, The Pink Boa was a sanctuary of self-expression and liberation. Stepping through its doors, patrons were transported into a realm where boundaries dissolved and inhibitions melted away in the pulsating rhythm of music and movement. I also had black and white films playing in the background with no sound: Bette Davis, people like that. So if you came on your own and you were a bit nervous, you had something to watch, something to take you away from the moment. I thought that was a good idea.

For six unforgettable months, The Pink Boa ignited the imaginations of all who dared to venture within, and its neon-lit corridors echoed with the laughter and camaraderie of a community united by acceptance and celebration of diversity. Here, performers dazzled with their artistry and graceful movements, weaving tales of empowerment and defiance against societal norms.

Escorting, strip-joints, lap-dancing... if there was no call for it we would be out of business. It is just a service, a personal service, a public service! I do think the girls who work in this industry should be looked after better and not be frowned upon, because as long as they are treating the customers correctly and they are respectful in themselves, there is no harm. We never phoned people up and said, 'You've got to come to see us.' You phoned us and said, 'I would like to come to see you.'

Though its time was fleeting, The Pink Boa left an indelible mark on the landscape of London's nightlife, a testament to the power of courage, creativity and inclusivity. As its doors closed for the last time, I hoped that at least The Pink Boa's legacy would endure, a beacon of inspiration for those who dared to challenge conventions and embrace the full spectrum of human expression.

The idea was that people could come along as a guy and then get dressed to look like a lady, have a dance, have some food and a lap dance if they wanted. People could meet a friend there or make arrangements to meet with someone beforehand, and then get dressed. It was like a one-stop and people were able to do everything in one place. That was the idea, but getting the right dancers proved to be very difficult, as you didn't want a big, hairy bum in your face (well, most people didn't, but there's no accounting for taste).

In 2015, I met a guy called Anthony; at least, I think that was his name. He was outside the club, The WayOut, where I used to go every so often, although not every week at this point. This particular week I'd decided to go just for the sake of going out and I had a jumper on and some unexciting trousers – blue, flowery things – and I had to go across the road, as the venue changed every so often. When I got there, I'd said to the guy at the reception, 'The WayOut's not here, is it?'

'No,' he replied, so I'd turned around and crossed the road, only to encounter an older man; a very tall, skinny TV, with red lipstick all over her face and a cheap, platinum blonde wig. She asked me how to find the club so I said she could follow me in, and then I went to the bar to get a drink. I first saw Anthony sitting next to this TV, so I decided to sit down next to her too, at the table. We were talking, but I couldn't really understand what she was saying. because she was drunk. Anthony, however, turned out to be smart, older, and well-educated, so by the end of the evening, we exchanged phone numbers.

I called him the next day or the day after, I can't remember exactly, but it was a big mistake as he turned out to be a psychopathic lying piece of rubbish! After weeks of flirtatious conversation, Anthony asked me out properly and I gladly accepted. In those early days, he wooed me with tales of rubbing elbows with celebrities and living a life of unbelievable luxury. He claimed his exclusive circle of friends included the notorious Kray twins, notorious gangsters who once ruled London's criminal underworld, and according to Anthony, he also socialised with politicians, diplomats and elite businessmen on a regular basis. I saw no concrete evidence of these connections, but Anthony described the marble foyers and penthouse parties in such sensuous detail I could almost taste the champagne and caviar.

To this day, I don't know whether his name was Anthony or Brian, and I still don't even know where he lives as he never took me there. He always had an excuse for everything, but he did have some very nice cars: a handmade Mercedes and a very large Bentley at one point, both of which I was lucky enough to drive, as he put me on the insurance. I stopped working when I was with Anthony, so it meant that I was living on my savings.

He claimed that the insurance would not allow me to go to his six-bedroom home in Saltwood, near Hythe, as he had a great deal of diamonds there. After a while, I stopped asking, although I always wondered how someone so plugged into London's rich and powerful didn't have a single photo of a famous friend or even himself at a society event. Nothing in our relationship added up anymore.

Sinking into depression, I stopped taking calls from old friends who still cared for my well-being and Anthony insisted these people from my past were holding me back, keeping me mired in mediocrity instead of ascending to my true station. So, isolated from anyone able to siphon the poison Anthony poured into my psyche daily, the gaslighting took hold.

Quickly I was questioning my own recollections and judgement: ripe fruit for Anthony's picking.

We started having problems with Blossom next door after a while, and some of the problems were caused by him, but I was also having problems with the landlord who wanted to put the rent up. I insisted that the flat had to be upgraded before I would pay any more, but that caused problems, and I started getting a bit down because Anthony was promising me all sorts of things and nothing was happening. I felt something was wrong, nothing felt quite right, and one evening I drank an awful lot and took some pills. I cannot remember specifically as it was all a bit of a blur, but I do remember calling an ambulance myself.

The first transsexual lap dancing club in Europe. It lasted less than a year. Very difficult to get the right girls 2013

This was my transsexual lap dancing club first in Europe. Pink Boa

Anthony, this is the only photo I have psychopath and liar. This is Beaulieu car museum, one of the few good days.

CHAPTER NINETEEN: UNUSUAL HOMES AND CURIOUS KINKS

They took me to the hospital once again, but this time, when I had just been discharged and still wasn't feeling 100%, I got back to find that the landlord was trying to kick the front door in. I had to drag the tumble dryer to the front of the house and jam the door closed, which was not a good moment in my life and I realised I had to move. Anthony lived in Hythe, so he told me, on Saltwood Hill, so when I saw a mobile home for rent, in Maidenhead somewhere, I drove straight there. There were a few mobile homes in a row with a lot of different types of other homes and I soon realised it was a gypsy camp. It seemed to be OK at first, moving in with all my stuff, especially as I didn't have a lot of things with me anyway, having left a lot behind.

The chair that I once lived in was very old and tatty now, so it was basically just me, a small assortment of bits and bobs, and Pearl, my French Bulldog, who I still own (Benji, my beautiful Chihuahua, had passed away by this point). Everything seemed to be OK, and Anthony came around once or twice a week. We'd get in his car and drive round and round, going nowhere, just driving, which I never really understood, but that's what we used to do for some reason.

Unfortunately, after a short while, the power suddenly went off in the gypsy camp, in the middle of winter, and never came back on. The fuses couldn't take the amount of power going through them because of the cold and if everyone put their heaters on, it just shut down. One of the gypsy brothers who was renting the mobile homes hadn't paid the electric bills which didn't help, and on top of that, another brother had put an axe through the cables! We were out of electricity for three weeks and had to manage on just gas and candles, but Anthony wasn't a great deal of help.

I used to charge my phone up in the car during the day, watch a programme on my phone and then go to bed, but life was muddy and dirty and I remember feeling very unsafe. I knew before long that I couldn't stay there anymore, so I looked for somewhere else and finally found another mobile home in Battle, in someone's garden! When I went to have a look, it was in the lady's front garden, although it was a big garden, as she had a small holding which was clean, safe and a thousand times better than the gypsy camp.

She had a washing machine I could borrow, I had electric bottled gas and everything I needed at the time, so I stayed there for the next five years, which I can hardly believe! The first winter I was there was the time of what was being called the Beast from the East, and for five days my living room was minus six and the curtains were frozen to the windows! Everything was frozen up, so it was a total nightmare, and true to form, Anthony hardly came around at all.

My brain was telling me something was desperately wrong with Anthony by this time, and I knew by then that he was a lying piece of rubbish and that I should get rid of him, but he was very manipulative and very clever. And then I started running out of money. I literally had no money left as I'd used up all my credit cards, and I had no cash left apart from a mere £50.

I had a huge argument with him and basically told him to go away, but soon after, he called me asking to meet up one more time to see if we could make things good again. I met him at a café in Kent that summer, but when I got out of the car, he frisked me down to see if I had been wired by the police. It seems like I'm making it up, but no, he frisked me because he believed I was working for the London mob. We had something to eat, but I couldn't eat. I couldn't even swallow. I couldn't do anything at all, so I basically just left as I couldn't stand looking at him anymore, which I'm glad to say was the end of it.

Anthony was 80, and I don't know why someone of that age had to be such a liar. I'd planned the design of a whole house he promised me in Cuba, but he left me penniless, and I had to start escorting again to get money, to survive once again, but by the time Covid-19 came along, luckily, I had enough money saved so I could get by. I walked the dog to get out and about, but Covid didn't really worry me. I just missed my escort work.

I started doing a bit of house cleaning but that did my back in and every penny I earned was spent on the osteopath, so, after a while, I carried on escorting. It was a bit difficult as I was still in a mobile home in someone's garden but I didn't have busloads of people, and it was literally one by one.

BLOOD, SWEAT AND SUSPENDERS

I did have one client when I was in the mobile home in Battle; a very strange person who sometimes used to turn up with a piece of paper for me to read out exactly what to do and say, but I'm not an actress, so that was difficult. One day, he turned up with a bag of stinging nettles and some garden gloves. I was glad that I wore the gloves as he got the stinging nettles all round his genitals! He seemed to enjoy it... Another time, he tied up his genitals so tight that they went black and I had to hit them with a hair brush which made them bleed. I was slightly distressed about that, although he wasn't...

It was difficult to find my home at night, as there was no street lighting, but I then decided to do some touring work in other places which generated a lot more money and was easier in a way. I went to Cardiff, Southampton, Northampton, Leicester, Bournemouth and Poole, and I did quite a lot of work in Slough.

CHAPTER TWENTY: LIVING AND LEARNING

After being in the mobile home for five years and more or less working about three and a half years from there, I encountered a policeman who lived on the corner and didn't like my landlady (although I don't know why as she was lovely). He, however, was not lovely and started causing problems for her; all sorts of silly little things. On top of that, he must have scoured the internet and found me on a site, but you don't just come across me by typing something in, so he must have been pretty determined. If I'd known he was so interested in me, I'd have given him a signed photograph! My landlady, Leslie, didn't know what I had been doing, so it was slightly embarrassing when the council came round saying that my customers had been knocking on this policeman's door, but that was utter lies as I always used to go out and meet them, or if they knew where I was, they knew how to get in. He was there to make trouble, but in the long run, it turned out well.

I found myself a lovely, ground floor apartment in St Leonards in December 2022, with a garden, and I'm still very good friends with Leslie, who let me live in her own front garden for five years. I still work at 64 years old, although I've cut my work down now to just two weeks of the month touring the whole of England, and I've still got Pearl and now Dotty, my little Chihuahua.

Touring around England sometimes has its problems, especially in long traffic jams on the motorways, but when you get to a certain age and you need a wee, you need a wee! I do have a bottle in the car so I have had to push the seat right back, pull my clothes down and hope and pray that a lorry doesn't go past so I can wee in the bottle before the traffic starts moving. So yes, I'm ambidextrous. I can do everything: Wee AND drive!

I have some very good friends in St Leonards, including Caroline, Gordon and her lovely mother, Margaret, and I've also met someone nice called Andrew. He must be a saint to put up with me as he knows that I'm still unable to have sex with someone I have feelings for, but even so, we're happy and the future's looking bright.

*

I hope my story inspires others to take ownership of their own lives despite straying from society's expectations. While much is beyond our control, we do have power over our most important choices – how we spend our time and whether we sacrifice conformity to be our true selves. I've learnt the hard way that denying my inner light only leads to emptiness.

Of course, I have regrets. I've experienced cruelty, apathy and greed, and I've caused harm to others in my own pursuit of desire, but to anyone I've hurt, I offer my deepest apologies. If I could turn back time, I would act from a place of greater wisdom and compassion.

I hope those who read my story can empathise rather than judge my shortcomings, as true beauty lies not in perfection, but in emerging from our darkest days. We are all a blend of light and shadow, but choosing the light gives our lives meaning, even throughout the struggles.

To all who have supported me along the way, thank you. Your kindness kept me anchored in times of uncertainty, and to those who offered me sanctuary during the storms, I am forever grateful. Though we may all feel alone at times, there are always hands reaching out to help if we're willing to accept them.

Though unconventional, my story raises questions of identity, purpose and fulfilment, but each of us must find our own answers in the end. I hope I continue to find patience and inner wisdom along the way, but I'm starting to believe it when I say: I am enough, we are all enough, and none of us has to be alone; except Phil, but he's a twat…

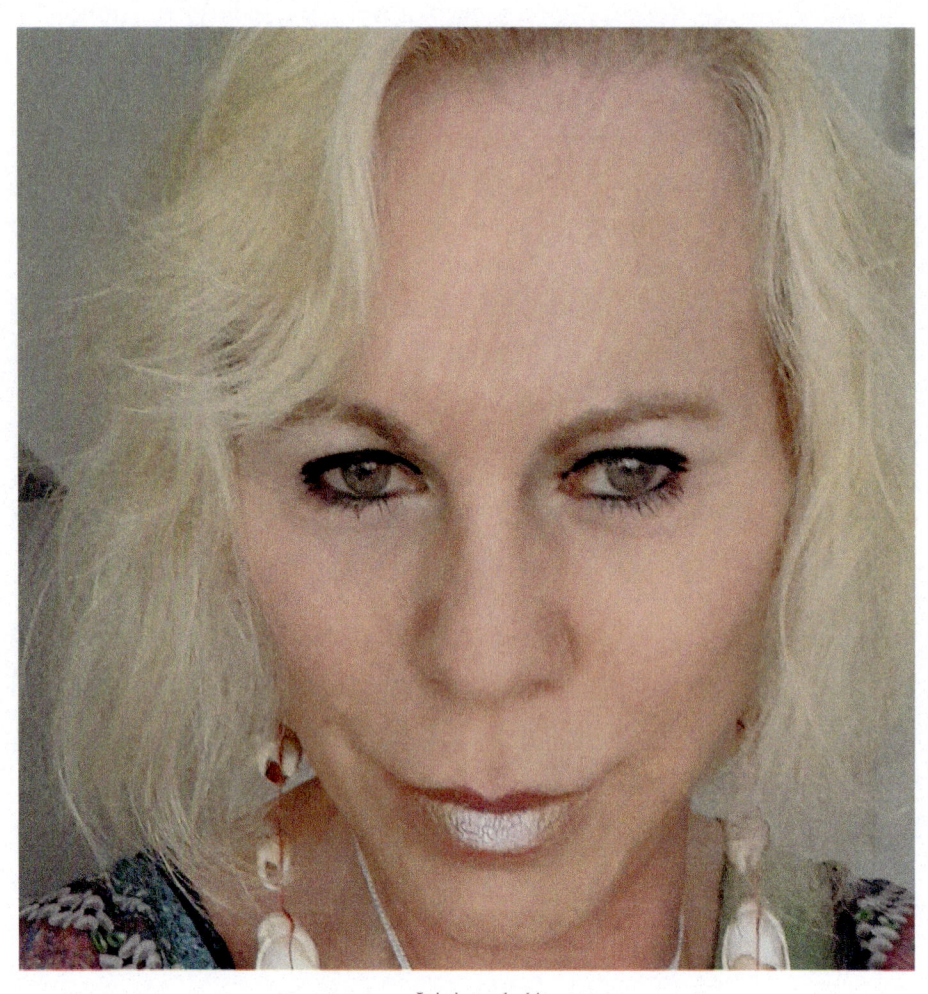

It is just a look!

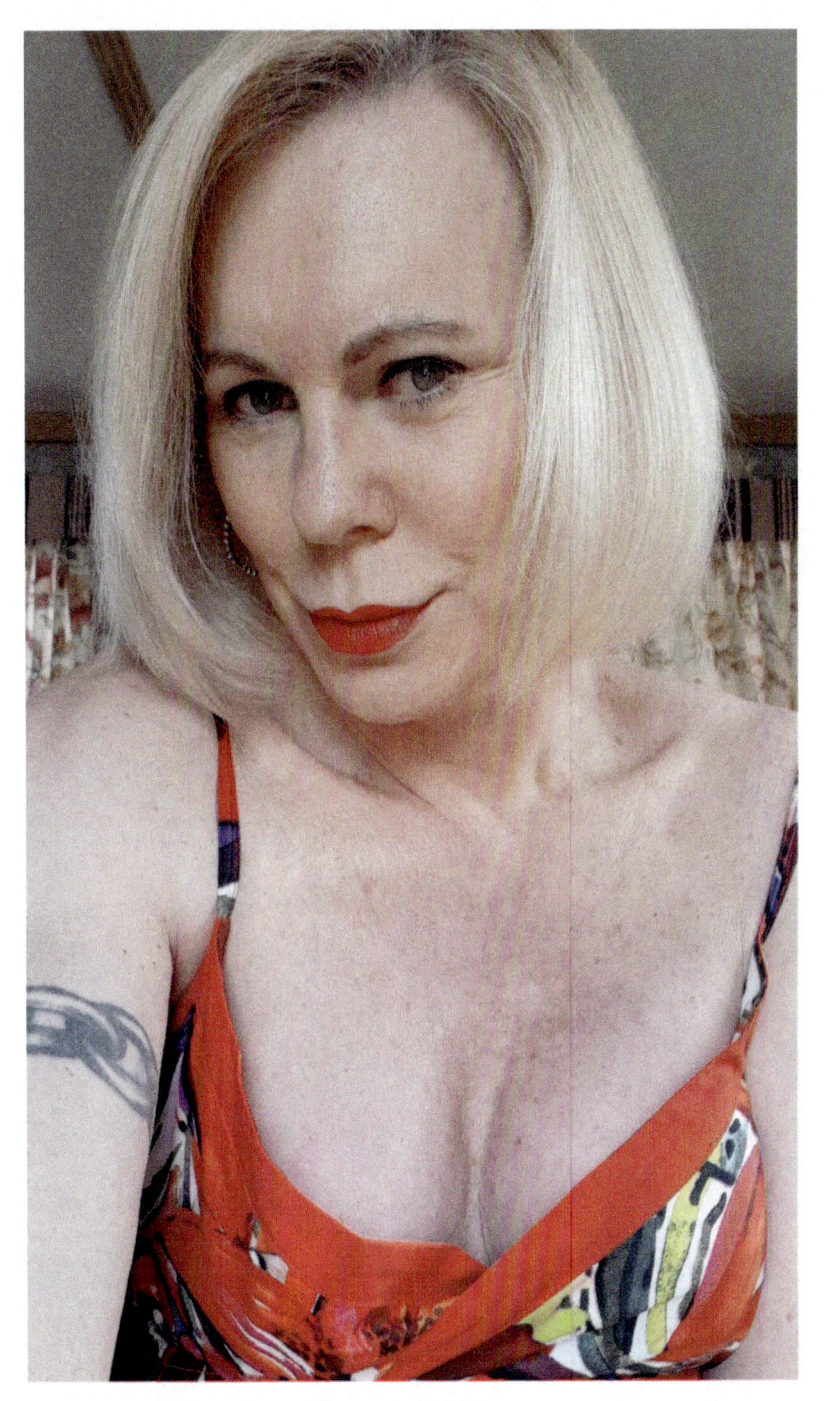

Then another look XX

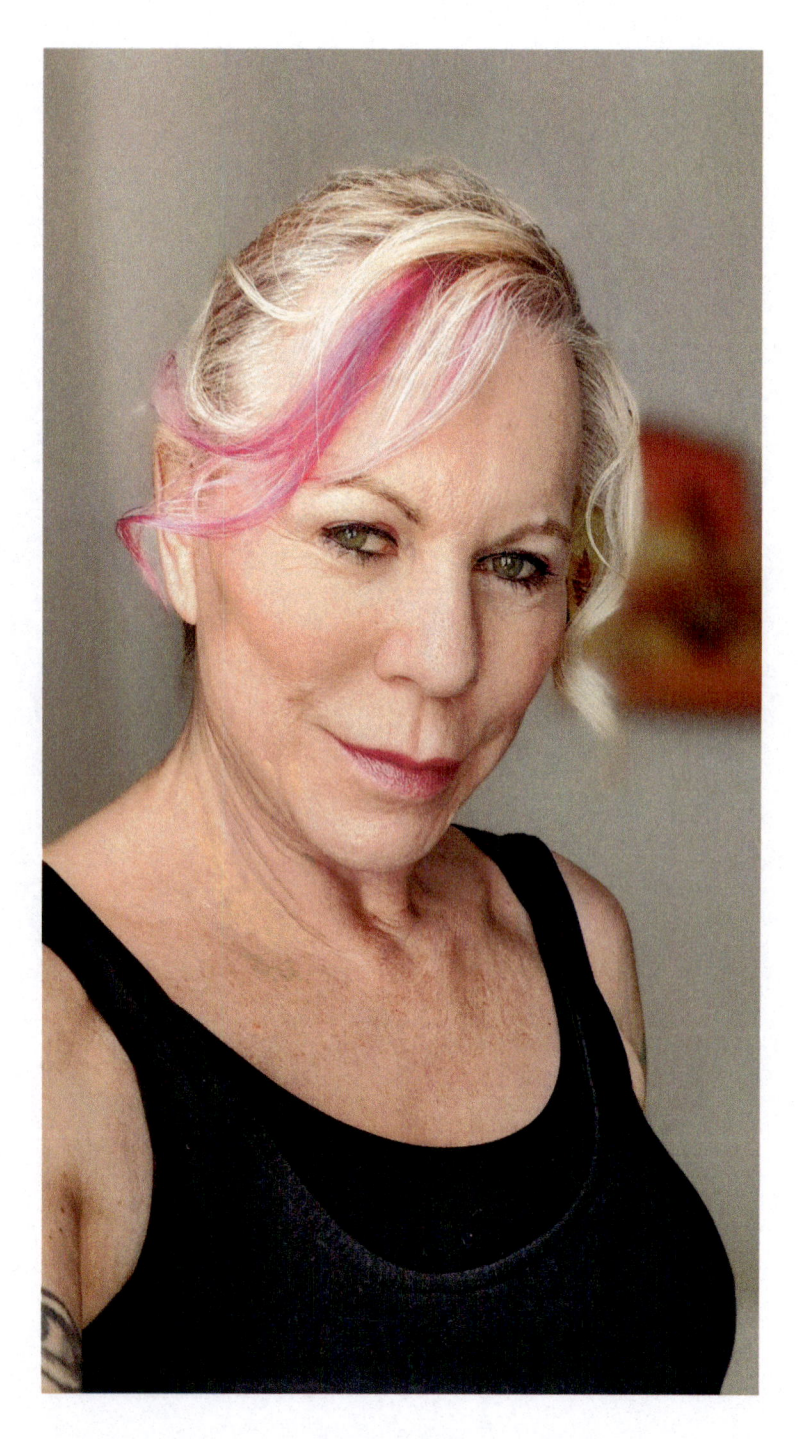

2023 new look, you may want to stop, but you have to keep going. Everyday is a new one.

Friends are important as I don't have family. Yourself, that's the most important. I lost myself twice, never again.

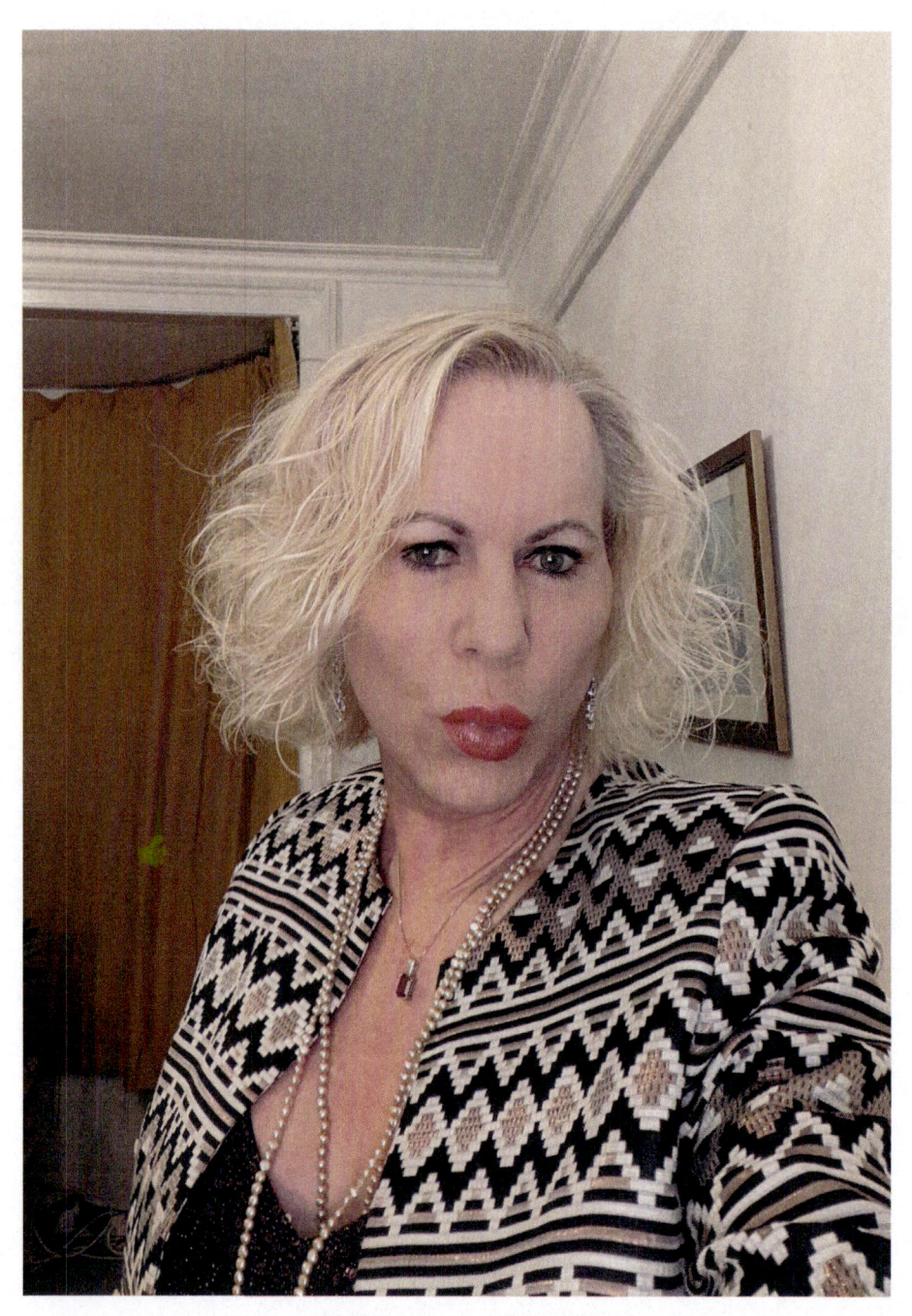

That's me now, 64 in 2024, XXXXX

Story Terrace

Printed in Great Britain
by Amazon